MW00468772

THE HOMILETICAL BEAT

Gene Lowry has been helping preachers to "do time" in the pulpit for a generation now. In *The Homiletical Beat* he continues his unapologetic defense of narrative preaching and defends it against critics who continue to confuse it with simply "telling stories in the pulpit." As both a master of the jazz piano and preaching, Lowry refuses to play the gospel melody with only one hand. Read this book for the full effect of the musicality of grace.

—Rev. Dr. Robin R. Meyers is senior minister of Mayflower United Church of Christ in Oklahoma City, professor of rhetoric at Oklahoma City University, and the author of *The Underground Church: Reclaiming the Subversive Way of Jesus.*

As a good jazz musician takes us ever deeper into the complexities of melody and harmony before finally coming to resolution, so Gene Lowry—jazz musician turned homiletician—takes us ever deeper into understandings of narrative, plot, and orality as they relate to preaching. Key themes in Lowry's previous works are lifted up here, but after Lowry's expansion and improvisation around those themes, we emerge with a much deeper appreciation for his homiletical music and its nuances.

—Leonora Tubbs Tisdale, Yale Divinity School

Taking its cues from Aristotle and Louis Armstrong, *The Homiletical Beat* shows how sermons can come to life when their ideas are harnessed to a narrative sequence. Freshly improvising on the themes of the New Homiletic he helped compose and conduct, Gene Lowry compellingly reprises the sermonic movement from complication to resolution—and does so in service to the surprising and startling God of the Bible.

—James F. Kay, Princeton Theological Seminary

THE HOMILETICAL BEAT

WHY ALL SERMONS ARE NARRATIVE

EUGENE L. LOWRY

Abingdon Press
Nashville

The Homiletical Beat
Why All Sermons Are Narrative

Copyright © 2012 by Eugene L. Lowry

All rights reserved.
No part of this work may be reproduced or transmitted in any form or by any means, electronic or mechanical, including photocopying and recording, or by any information storage or retrieval system, except as may be expressly permitted by the 1976 Copyright Act or in writing from the publisher. Requests for permission can be addressed to Permissions, The United Methodist Publishing House, P.O. Box 801, 201 Eighth Avenue South, Nashville, TN 37202-0801, or emailed to permissions@umpublishing.org.

Library of Congress Cataloging-in-Publication Data has been requested.

ISBN 978-1-4267-5143-1

Scripture quotations unless otherwise indicated are from the New Revised Standard Version of the Bible, copyright 1989, Division of Christian Education of the National Council of the Churches of Christ in the United States of America. Used by permission. All rights reserved.

Scripture quotations marked NASB are taken from the *New American Standard Bible®*, Copyright © 1960, 1962, 1963, 1968, 1971, 1972, 1973, 1975, 1977, 1995 by The Lockman Foundation. Used by permission. (www.Lockman.org)

Scripture quotations marked KJV are from the King James or Authorized Version of the Bible.

Excerpt marked Jerusalem Bible is from THE JERUSALEM BIBLE, copyright © 1966 by Darton, Longman & Todd, Ltd. and Doubleday, a division of Random House, Inc. Reprinted by Permission.

Scripture quotations marked NIV are taken from the Holy Bible, NEW INTERNATIONAL VERSION®. Copyright © 1973, 1978, 1984 by International Bible Society. All rights reserved throughout the world. Used by permission of International Bible Society.

Scripture quotations marked NEB are from *The New English Bible.* © The Delegates of the Oxford University Press and The Syndics of the Cambridge University Press 1961, 1970. Reprinted by permission.

Scripture quotations marked RSV are from the Revised Standard Version of the Bible, copyright 1952 [2nd edition, 1971] by the Division of Christian Education of the National Council of the Churches of Christ in the United States of America. Used by permission. All rights reserved.

Scripture quotations marked JBP are from J. B. Phillips, The New Testament in Modern English. Copyright © 1962 edition, published by HarperCollins.

Figure on page 19 is Figure 6.1 Metrical Matrix from Jeremy S. Begbie, *Theology, Music and Time* copyright © 2000 by Cambridge University Press. Reprinted with the permission of Cambridge University Press.

Excerpts from Thomas Troeger in ch. 2 are from *Imagining a Sermon by Thomas Troeger*, © 1990 Abingdon Press.

12 13 14 15 16 17 18 19 20 21—10 9 8 7 6 5 4 3 2 1

MANUFACTURED IN THE UNITED STATES OF AMERICA

To

Carl Michalson

H. Grady Davis

Fred B. Craddock

CONTENTS

PREFACE

This writing is an outgrowth of two recent lectureships: the Lyman Beecher Lectures of 2009, at Yale University Divinity School, and the William Self Lectures on Preaching of 2011, at McAfee School of Theology, Mercer University.

To be asked to deliver these two prestigious lectureships is to prompt both thrill and trembling. One not seriously intimidated ought not be asked. Moreover, noting that the invitation to Yale was sent by Dean Leander Keck, the welcome to New Haven provided by Dean Harold W. Attridge, and the invitation to Mercer/McAfee proffered by Dean R. Alan Culpepper—all three world-renowned biblical scholars—is actually to summon more than your very best!

Our arrival at both Yale and McAfee revealed the kind of warm graciousness already evidenced by those who had the responsibility of supervising the preparation necessary for the events to happen. Grace Pauls, assistant to Dean Attridge, made us feel at home even before we arrived—indeed, becoming a friend in the process. Diane Frazier, assistant to Dean Culpepper, embodied the art of shepherding a lectureship event into actuality. Homiletical colleagues Nora Tisdale and

Tom Troeger at Yale and Peter Rhea Jones and Brett Younger at McAfee provided extraordinary, collegial welcome—all going out of their way to structure ongoing hospitality throughout our visits. The staff, faculty, and students all made Sarah and me feel included in their particular world of work.

The process of turning these lectures into a book was more complicated than any of my previous projects. It was Dale Krebbs, webmaster, consultant, and lifetime friend, whose technical expertise was crucial in the work of transposing my style of lecturing into print-based form. And it was he who provided remarkable musical editing of the recording of the second lecture/chapter, available by technical links. My fellow musicians who traveled to Yale—Mac McCune, trumpeter, and Carlos Summers, trombonist—made "Encountering the Aristotle Blues" come alive. The content of the lectures has been added to, subtracted from, edited, and translated from the mode of orality into a somewhat modified mode of literality.

It is wonderful to be welcomed again to Abingdon Press by Paul Franklyn, Associate Publisher. It was Dr. Franklyn who brought Senior Leadership Editor Len Wilson and me together for the editorial process. Len was a wonderful editor, clear about the particular purposes of this writing, sharp about needed clarity of expression, and open to the ongoing dialogue necessary for the decision-making process. I am particularly grateful for how he found a way for the book cover to become a parabolic statement about what the book is all about. As always, Sarah is my careful critic and my love.

In my homiletical journey, I have often presumed I was actually providing some basic novelty of thought to the subject—only to discover otherwise. (In fact, I once thought I had invented the plot's "principle of reversal" only to find out that it had been stolen by Aristotle some time back.)

Hence, it is a joy to name three incredible mentors for this book's dedication. Each of them has graced me preveniently in the fullest sense of previous and anticipatory.

For example, it has finally come to me that my interest in narrative was first piqued quite without my knowledge by Professor Carl Michalson of Drew University School of Theology. I understood clearly that he was teaching us Systematic Theology—and that he was a genius at it. But he was doing far more than that. I was totally unaware that he was also teaching me what it means to work narratively. I did notice that he never used any notes when he lectured—or when preaching. It has taken several decades to discover that he was actually modeling for me the narrative world that later I would attempt to offer others.

Long after I had ceased using H. Grady Davis's *Design for Preaching* as a course text, it finally dawned on me that an underlying principle of his, quietly named in the middle of the book, actually is central to all preaching. (Indeed, some of this discovery has happened to me in the last five years.) It must have been looking for me for a very long time.

I will never forget the moment in my earliest days of teaching at Saint Paul School of Theology, when someone remarked that "you must be familiar with the work of Fred Craddock, who has written a book about the subject you are discussing."

Well, I considered my point of view to be a new perspective on preaching. "What's the name?" I asked. And my early days of disappointment—of falsely believing I had actually provided a new direction for preaching all on my own—turned to absolute joy in the privilege of sitting at the feet of mentor Fred B. Craddock.

Carl Michalson, H. Grady Davis, and Fred B. Craddock—the debt is enormous.

INTRODUCTION

The term *narrative preaching* as affirmed in this writing does not refer to a subset option for some sermons. It is not simply a name for some homiletical genre thought particularly suitable for the use of stories, or for certain kinds of subject matter. Rather, it is the fundamental context for—indeed the underlying modus operandi of—the homiletical event we call the sermon. H. Grady Davis established this rationale with simple yet profound clarity over fifty years ago. Although he did not utilize the term *narrative*, he described it when he said:

> A sermon is not static like a painting. A painting shows itself
> as a whole in a single instant. Not only its entire composition,
> all its subjects and their arrangement, but all its minutest de-
> tails stand there together, fixed in their intended relation to
> one another and to the whole. It is a visible design, complete
> and static. The eye takes it all in at once. A sermon is never
> like that, never has the objective completeness of a picture or
> a building.[1]

Indeed, a sermon exists within a wholly different category. Joining the sermon in this other genre are events provided by music, drama, and cinema. Fundamentally these are not visible designs set in space, but temporal arts functioning in time. Truth is, as Davis explained it:

> A sermon is like music, not music in the score but in the live performance, where bar is heard after bar, theme after theme, and never all at once. A sermon is like a play, not the printed book but the action on a stage, which moves from a first act through a second to a third, and the drama is never [experienced] . . . all at once. A sermon is like a story told aloud, where each sentence has gone forever into the past before the next is spoken.[2]

Here, the ear is primary, not the eye—not so much fixed in space as carried along in time—moment by moment, beat by beat. And if you miss this fundamental difference between these separable categories of function—between *all-at-once* and *moment-by-moment*—the sermon is robbed of its very nature. Simple as that.

It is important to observe now that language regarding "mouth to ear as contrasted with hand to eye," as utilized in this writing, ought not be construed in an unthinking literalism. The underlying issue here has to do with the difference between temporal sequence and the all-at-once. Hence, in the case of those who are deaf, as Stephen H. Webb puts it, "The muscles of the limbs take the place of the muscles of the throat."[3] So too, the eyes function as the ears. Again, the contrast is between the set and the in-motion. Likewise, those at the opera who do not speak Italian have subtitles in order to understand the operatic voices and hence interpret the movements on stage. And the opera moves on from note to note and theme to theme.

No wonder H. Grady Davis went on to say: "If we wish to learn from other arts, we must learn from these arts based on a time sequence."[4] He even continued his observation about the connection with music by saying, "I must play [assertions] . . . as a musician plays . . . principal themes."[5] Davis was joined forty-six years later by Kirk Byron Jones, who in 2000 declared, "Musicians play notes; preachers play words."[6]

Presentations whose form is lined out *moment-by-moment* are narrative by definition. Presentations whose form occurs *all-at-once* are not. Musical presentations are narrative by form. A sculptural presentation is not. The primary medium of preaching is time, moving moment-by-moment. Hence, narrative is its primary form. This is what I mean when I speak of the narrative principle of preaching.

So it is that by means of this principle we keep time with the Word. This is what preaching is all about, and the exploration and explanation of this understanding was the primary purpose in both my Lyman Beecher Lectures at Yale in 2009, and the William Self Lectures at Mercer University /McAfee School of Theology in 2011, on which this book is based.

Chapter Two

THE THREE LEVELS OF NARRATIVITY

It's Sermon *Time.*

That's the right name for it. I have been calling attention to it by use of the term *narrative* for decades now. Sometimes I have employed the term *plotted preaching.* Other writers have differing terminology for similar commitments.

Fred Craddock once spoke of "inductive preaching," Lucy Rose moved toward "conversational preaching," David Buttrick preferred "plotted mobility," Charles Rice focused on "story preaching," and Henry Mitchell spoke of the sermonic route toward "celebration." Believing that several of us were on the same page—or at least on similarly concerned pages—Richard Eslinger featured five of us as participating in what David James Randolph once coined as the "New Homiletic." Eslinger considered the new homiletical movement the "Copernican Revolution in homiletics."[1]

So at the heart of the matter, what is it precisely that in spite of several key differences joins these similar theorists together? Clearly, I believe, it is that all of us have focused on the crucial concern about *sequence*. Whether Mitchell is moving toward the sermonic celebration, Buttrick pressing toward a new corporate consciousness, Rose putting matters into an ongoing conversation, Rice telling a story, or Craddock talking about the necessity of anticipation within the sermon—all are talking about *temporal sequence* as basic to the preaching event. I call it *narrativity*—not an optional choice for the sermon, but the central thread, the formative principle of what the sermon is.

Level One: Narrative as Temporal Modality

H. Grady Davis not only said, "The proper design of a sermon is a movement in time," he also said, "it begins at a given moment, it ends at a given moment, and it moves through the intervening moments one after another."[2]

At first reading I thought that statement pretty obvious. Of course, when preachers first begin their message, they start talking, and pretty soon they get through with their message and stop talking—and indeed, they also talk in between those two points in time. But what seemed to me then an obvious observation, I now understand to be at the heart of Davis's utterly radical transformational gift to us. It has taken me a lifetime to even begin to absorb what this means. Indeed, the homiletical guild has focused on his other gifts to us—such as the "generative idea," the "union of substance and form," and the metaphor of a sermon imaged as a tree—and somehow this more radical germinal gift has not fully been harvested.

Indeed, the idea sort of shows up almost unannounced in the middle of the book, in a chapter on "Continuity: Nature and Types."[3]

Davis continued, "A sermon is not a manuscript, not a paper outline simple or elaborate, not a sketch. . . . A sermon is a continuity of sounds, looks, gestures which follow one another in time."[4] I believe that we in the homiletical community have yet to grasp fully the enormous implications of this "simple" statement. Otherwise, we would have learned to speak not so much about sermon *points* as about sermon *steps*.

And how might we identify just how radical these ideas are? The first step is to notice some images that many preachers tend to use when talking about their sermons—images spoken without apparent reflection about the unspoken assumptions that lie underneath. In fact, sometimes this kind of language is used by those who are teachers of preaching!

I have found that when preachers converse with other preachers about the sermon, often they do not speak about time, let alone about time's continuity. It is as though the sermon is sensed as an object in space. By Friday of the week, you may have heard somebody discuss his or her preparation for Sunday's sermon. When asked how she is doing with her preparation, she may say, "Well, I think I am about to get it together." *Together?* It—*and*—together? What do preachers mean by "get it together"? The terms *it* and *together* do not belong together in such a sentence. But the underlying assumptive image is clear: *Space*—something like the image in Sangster's *Craft of Sermon Construction,* and in Nichols' *Building the Word.*

7

And it has a corollary lexicon to match—a thing constructed, like on a corner lot; parts that get organized, like a jigsaw puzzle; ideas that are assembled, like in a car plant. Actually, the Lyman Beecher lecturer of 1908, William Herbert Perry Faunce, said that we do not want "sermons built up as a carpenter builds a row of houses."[5] Yet too often it is space that seems to be the underlying assumptive image regarding the sermon.

Instead, H. Grady Davis spoke of time and, rather than referring to outlines, spoke of forms of continuity. He knew that the sermon participates primarily in time, not space—is not *all-at-once* in place, but appears *movingly-in-sequence*, beat after beat. No wonder he said, "If we wish to learn from other arts, we must learn from these arts based on a time sequence."[6]

All of which is to say again that whatever we do in the pulpit *is* narrative. That is, its presence is not only facilitated in the passage of time—its existence is *within* time sequence. That's where it is—nowhere else. A sermon is an ordered form of moving time—the narrative principle of preaching at work. This is only the first level of consideration, but its recognition is crucial before proceeding further.

As Toni Craven, Professor of Hebrew Scripture at Brite Divinity School, named it, we are dealing with temporal sequence, which is her definition of narrative. It is the medium of our work. It is the given in McLuhan's sense, the context of whatever other variables are chosen. Therefore, your sermon next Sunday will be narrative no matter what. That is, the sermon will in fact move from beginning to end in the medium of time. Period.

The sermon—whether deductive or inductive, whether image-based or logically driven, story or declaration, linear or episodal, improvised or manuscript in the corporate setting of worship—is an experience in timely form, as *recital.* It is not presented all-at-once like painting or sculpture. It lives in time like music, cinema, and poetry. This fact is primary to preaching, not secondary or optional.

In presenting both the Lyman Beecher and the William Self Lectures, the basis for this work, I used a piano to explain further. I played all the single melody notes of a well-known hymn of the church, slowly and without any rhythm. I began with middle C: C C C C C C, D D D, F F F F F F F F F F F, G G G, A A A A A A A A A, C C C. The last three Cs were an octave above middle C. Then I asked the audience to name the hymn of which these are the melody notes. Of course none was able to answer. I feigned disappointment, saying,

> I am surprised that you are so unfamiliar with the hymnody of the church. Well, that was "Amazing Grace" . . . yes it was. . . . Well, I have a confession to make. I did not play the notes in sequence!
>
> Now, you have every right to say "if you don't play the notes in sequence, how dare you call it anything, let alone Amazing Grace?" You know, those thirty-five notes—six Cs, three Ds, eleven Fs, and so on. . . . Somebody could compose another song altogether, using the same thirty-five notes—but occurring in a different order. So I decided to do just that—and composed a different song made up of exactly the same thirty-five notes—but in a different sequence. I have titled it "Unamazing Grace." I will play it now.

I played my new song, and then remarked, "Now, please understand that I do know the proper sequence for 'Amazing Grace.' " I then played it in a jazz idiom in order to make it clear that when you change the sequence of the notes, you are playing a different song. And when you change the sequence of your words in the pulpit, you are preaching a different sermon.

No wonder Fred Craddock once said that *"how* one preaches is to a large extent *what* one preaches."[7] Or, as Ciardi and Williams expressed it in *How Does a Poem Mean?*: "The way in which it means is what it means."[8] And in large part, the *how of it* depends on decisions about temporal sequence. (The other companion component of sermonic form has to do with language choice—to which we will move later in the next section.)

So why is it that such different worlds of presentational shape as between static all-at-once forms (for example, painting and sculpture) and moment-by-moment forms (for example, music and preaching) play such a small role in homiletical theory? How can it be that this clear and profound aspect of the work of H. Grady Davis seems to have been allowed to drift to the periphery in our work? I believe it has to do with a linguistic definitional confusion.

I confess that even I who have been advocating "narrative preaching" through several books and decades appear to have been content to view "narrative preaching" as an option—although for me the preferred option. Yet what H. Grady Davis declared was that the sermon, viewed generically, is simply one of several presentational forms of art that happen by means of temporal sequence, rather than all at once. The elemental fact of temporal sequence in the sermon is one manifestation of the narrative arts. How is it then possible for the subject to be considered otherwise?

I believe it has happened by means of confusion about the difference between the terms *narrative* and *story*. For a long time I have battled against presuming those terms to be synonymous. The matter came clearer to me in preparation for the Beecher and the Self Lectures. It was colleague Thomas Long who presented the issue so clearly—albeit perhaps unintentionally. Long preceded me in presenting both the Lyman Beecher and the William Self Lectures on preaching. The issue emerges in his first lecture in both lectureships.

Finding Clarity about the Terms Narrative *and* Story

Long's first lectures both at Yale and Mercer form the beginning of their written form published as *Preaching from Memory to Hope*. On page 2 of the very first chapter the banner across the page announces the opening theme: "The Rise of Narrative Preaching."[9] And on the very next page he mentions three writers he believes are central to the subject of narrative preaching. H. Grady Davis is the first theorist chosen. Long described Davis as the one who "argued that preachers should no longer think of sermons as didactic arguments with orderly points but as living organisms, moving, dynamic, growing; in other words, a preacher should imagine a sermon more like a short story than a legal brief."[10] Said Long: "It felt like a fresh breeze," and "became the most popular preaching textbook in American seminaries for fifteen years."[11]

The second featured writer was, of course, Fred B. Craddock.

Rightly calling Craddock's *As One Without Authority* "the most influential monograph on preaching in our time," he focused on Craddock's calling preachers to "abandon the top-down, deductive, 'my thesis for this morning' approach to sermons in favor of suspenseful, inductive, narratives of discovery."[12] Of course he mentioned Craddock's Lyman Beecher Lectures of 1978, *Overhearing the Gospel,* with its focus on the work of Søren Kierkegaard.

Finally, and still on page 3, he turned to his third featured writer with the words, "In 1980, another teacher of preaching, Eugene Lowry, published the widely used and enormously influential preaching textbook *The Homiletical Plot . . .*"

Well, I was thrilled to be included on the same page with Davis and Craddock—until I read the last part of the sentence: ". . . *The Homiletical Plot,* which claimed. . . ." [Did I read that correctly? "Claimed"? Sounds like trouble ahead.] ". . . claimed that what really gets the juices going for hearers is not learning about ideas but resolving ambiguity, and thus good sermons should be built on the chassis of a narrative plot that moves sequentially from stirring up ambiguity to resolving it, from conflict to climax to denouement."[13]

Well, the last part of the sentence was on target, but frankly it was troubling that he seemed to be claiming that I wasn't really interested in dealing with ideas. In fact, his remark reminded me of a particular sentence I had used when asked by William H. Willimon and Richard Lischer to write the section on "Narrative Preaching" in the *Concise Encyclopedia of Preaching.* It was in that section that I stated the following: "A *narrative sermon* is any sermon in which the arrangement of ideas takes the form of a plot involving a strategic delay of the preacher's meaning."[14] I still consider that a reasonably clear description of the operative goal of good preaching. The phrase "arrangement of ideas" reflects my conviction for years now—even decades—that my work is intentionally geared toward helping preachers maximize the opportunity not only for engaging ideas, but more importantly, being engaged by those ideas. (We will explore the strategic dimension in the later description of the second narrative level of preaching.) I then turned to page 4 in Long's published form of the Beecher and Self Lectures.

At the very top of the page he cited another theoretical source with three editors, Steimle, Niedenthal, and Rice. They offered their definition for what a narrative sermon ought to be by asking this question:

> Is there an image adequate to shape the form, content, and style of preaching? If we had to say in a word or two, or in a picture, what preaching is and how it is done well, what would that phrase or picture be? . . . Let us consider the storyteller. . . . If we were pressed to say what Christian faith and life are, we could hardly do better than *hearing, telling, and living* a story. And if asked for a short definition of preaching, could we do better than *shared story*?[15]

On reading this passage, I began asking myself, *What is happening here?* I concluded that we just changed subjects. I read on, hoping that I might be incorrect. But Long continued, noting the "endless" varieties, "but all of them riffs on the notion that good preaching was somehow *story* shaped, *story* saturated, *story* driven" (italics added).[16] When the term shifted from narrative to story, that's when it became clear that we were

13

on an altogether different page and considering a differently defined subject.

Some might say, "Now wait a minute. He is using the term *story*; you use the term *narrative*. They are synonymous terms, are they not?" No, they are not synonymous terms at all. The subject somehow has shifted. Truth is, story and narrative denote overlapping categories. They are not totally separate categories, but overlapping ones, and if you do not watch out, the larger category will get swallowed up into the smaller category. In this case it is *narrative* that will get swallowed up inside *story*.

An analogy may be helpful to explain what I mean. I have often asked my students to respond orally to a single word I call out, telling them that when they hear the word to call back the first word that comes to mind. In such an exercise there are no wrong answers; the point is to experience the broad range of possible meanings. The word is: *medicine*.

The immediate responses I have experienced range from "prescription" on one end to the "practice of medicine" on the other. Other responses have been "yuck," "medical science," "doctor," "sick," "healing," and so on. If you look up the word *medicine* in a dictionary, the kind that begins first with the simplest definition and then moves toward the broadest, the first reference for medicine is "a substance used to treat disease." But that is not the end of the matter. Further definitions include "the science and art of sustaining or restoring health" and "the practice of medicine." In short, there is a very wide range of possible meanings for the term *medicine*.[17]

Now, suppose we were to agree that from now on, whenever we use the term *medicine,* it will mean "substance used to treat disease," or simply "prescription." That's it; nothing else. Who would agree with that stipulation? No one! The wide range of meanings is far too broad for such a limitation. And in fact, *prescription* is a particularly narrow choice—only a little piece among the many possibilities. It is a small possible subset of the category of *medicine.* Indeed, some doctors do not even prescribe drugs, because their particular branch of medicine does not call for it. Such a stipulation would not just reduce the category of *medicine,* it would collapse all of its broadly based meanings into the single possible subset category of prescriptions—nothing more!

This matter is precisely the issue in considering the categories of *narrative* and *story.* The question here has to do with what in fact is the most functionally appropriate meaning of the term *narrative preaching.*

If you look up a definition for the term *narrative* in the same kind of dictionary as mentioned before, you will find the first possibility as "something narrated—like a story." This is particularly so if an article is included (*a* or *the*). But, of course, then the further definitions reflect much broader matters. The second likely choice may be "the art or practice of narration," with synonyms suggested, such as plot, shape, movement, or unfolding pattern. A third definition may list adjectival/adverbial use, such as "narrative recital, narrative skills, narrative history," which presumes a relationship to the second definitional meaning of narrative art or practice. The category is broad. The question of utilization is whether you mean narrative as *example* or narrative as *form or shape*. As was the case for the term *medicine*, the term *narrative* is the broad category. *Story* is one possible subset. To presume that the terms are synonymous is to collapse the larger meaning into the smaller possible subset.

In Long's lectures and resultant publication, this very confusion continues. Very shortly the reader of *Preaching from Memory to Hope* will find a banner headline across page 7: "Narrative Preaching Faces the Critics,"[18] and notes that it "is catching it these days from the philosophers, from the theological right, middle, and left, and at multiple levels." But then we should observe how he defines the criticism:

> The theological right zings most sharply at the level of churchly practice: the telling of stories may ease minds and entertain the choir, but it doesn't build churches and extend the body of Christ.
>
> The middle has an educational complaint: the telling of stories may educe theological knowledge when it is already in place, but it doesn't supply it when it is not.
>
> For the theological left, the challenge is ethical. Storytelling enforces through coercion a monochromatic world upon the multihued experiences of others.[19]

He then concludes that what is at stake here philosophically are "assumptions about ethics and anthropology that undergird the whole storytelling enterprise."[20]

Note, however, how it is that the category of *narrative* has in fact been collapsed into the smaller category of *story*. I presume this happens unintentionally, not as a bait-and-switch strategy. And Long is not alone in not differentiating between narrative and story categories. He is joined by such writers as Richard Lischer, Charles Campbell, and John McClure.

What is noteworthy here is that if one refers to H. Grady Davis, Fred Craddock, or myself, the meaning is quite clear. For all three of us, use of the term *narrative* refers to the shape or pattern of narration. Davis said that the "proper design of a sermon is a movement in time."[21] One of the options of the "movement in time" design, he noted, is that of "story," but it is only one of five "organic forms" he discussed.[22]

A few years ago Fred Craddock explained what he understands a narrative sermon to be. He said, "Some people think that a narrative sermon is one that consists only of one long story. That is possible, but not likely. Others think a narrative sermon is one that is chock full of illustrations and stories end to end. That is possible but not likely. In fact, you can have a narrative sermon that does not include a single story."[23]

When I use the term *narrative sermon* or *narrative preaching* normatively, I refer to the arrangement of ideas that takes the form of a homiletical plot. Now, obviously, a parable of Jesus is a narrative or story. Such a story is easily formed into a narrative sermon. One can also take a text that is not itself in narrative form and yet strategically move it into effective narrative homiletical shape—a plot form. I am talking about the arrangement of ideas that happens by means of the human voice, moment-by-moment-by-moment.

Strangely, in an essay published over twenty-five years ago, Tom Long said, "Sermons cannot always be stories; they sometimes do not even include stories but they must always have plots, patterns of dynamic sequential elements."[24] That was his view in 1983, and seems to me exactly on target.

More recently, Fred Craddock had this to say about narrative preaching:

> The subject . . . is . . . narrative preaching, and not about stories that may or may not be components of the sermon. . . . Narrative moves from tension to resolution, from ambiguity to clarity, from what seems to be to what is, from guilt to grace, from death to life. Narrative, then, is the shape or movement of the sermon; it is not a piece of the sermon. Narrative describes the whole, not a component.[25]

So, as a musician plays notes into time—a sequenced narrative shape—so a preacher sends words into some kind of narratively principled sequence. We play the words into time, whispered into time, activating time, transforming time. Sunday after Sunday, time after time, beat after beat.

Note that at this level, our focus has been on the sheer temporal facticity of preaching, the first of the three levels of narratively principled preaching. Naturally, the next question is how, why, and with what effect? So we turn to the second level of preaching's narrativity.

Level Two: Narrative as Strategic Aim

When using time sequence as one's central category, the proper first question is how best to use the time given. What strategies should be employed and what potential variables are at play? Well, if you are a singer, it is good to sing on key. Speakers should stay on course, but what course will maximize our purpose? Craddock once said that, as preachers, "the goal is not to get something said but to get something heard."[26]

I am fascinated by the recent work of Jeremy Begbie, formerly of Cambridge and now at Duke—a man of numerous talents. He is a concert pianist, oboist, and conductor. He also is a theologian and has recently written the volume *Theology, Music and Time.* He says that music involves the twin elements of *tension* and *resolution.* And it happens in multiple forms. These he explains by means of a graphic design—small top half-circles on a line, and then with larger top-half circles on a second level that are wider than those on the lower line, and so on. The point is that tension/resolution occurs both at the point of short lengths of time and also at longer lengths of time, and finally even one sequence of tension/resolution that represents the whole sweep of the timely musical event. In short there are differing spans of multiple movements from tension to resolution.[27]

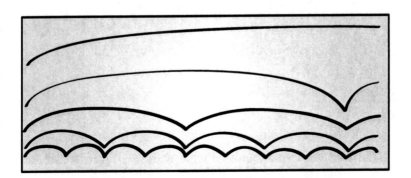

The Narrative Strategy of Tension-Resolution

Begbie is quick to clarify that his use of the term *tension* is not negative. Rather it has to do with "crucial anticipation." Indeed, "matters cannot be left where they are."[28] In fact he says that such anticipation creates a musical "meantime," an analogy to Paul's "foretaste" in Romans 8.[29] He is saying that by means of musical delay, "promise and fulfillment"[30] have a theological floor—from tension to resolution. It is a narrative strategy with theological roots.

One of the most fascinating sections of Begbie's work focuses on the remarkable difference between musical *composition* and musical *improvisation*. With strong affirmation, he turns to Christopher Small's startling comparison between the two:

> Western composed music is like a journey made by a composer who goes out, comes back from "out there," and tells us something, as best he can, of what it was like. . . . The journey may have been a long, arduous and fascinating one, and we may be excited, moved and even amused by it, but we cannot enter fully into the experience with him because the experience was over and he was safely home before we came to hear of it. . . . In improvising, on the other hand, the musician takes us with him on his journey of exploration.[31]

That profound insight revealed crisply for me the parallel situation for the experience of jazz. I have been fortunate to live in a great jazz city, Kansas City, and privileged to hear some of the best jazz artists in the entire country. But sometimes I have a problem in listening to a particularly wonderful group, one that has moved to becoming a particularly "tight" group—as it is called. The problem is that it is not improvising anymore. Returning to a subsequent performance I began hearing the same riffs as I heard a month ago, and before that, three months ago. No doubt the music is more finely honed, but it now lacks that component that most characterizes jazz—the element of improvisation. Earlier, when the musicians were beginning their work together, eyes flashed back and forth, one player waiting to hear what will soon come their way for response, receiving and giving, sharing in vulnerability, working against the risk of chaos. (One Kansas City musician spoke of the risk of improvisation as "falling off a cliff.") Those times were exciting, the music thrilling. But now when played over and over and over, the music is wonderful, perhaps even "more finely nuanced," and a lot more certain—but it will no longer take the breath away. The later performances were but composite "cloning" of prior experiences that now have become "secondhand." Diminished! And it is no longer jazz. *There is a difference between improvisation and memory, between spontaneous creativity and muscle-memory.*

When transferred to the subject of preaching, this difference is not hard to notice—everything else being equal—regarding the relative difference of narrative power between the African American preacher who is actually doing call and response improvisation in the Sunday service, with the somewhat lesser narrative power of a European American preacher whose intrapersonal improvisation stopped in the study on Saturday. (Again, everything else being equal.) It is with even less narrative power for a preacher who had no intrapersonal improvisation in the study to begin with (everything else being equal) and less power yet for one whose engagement in the study was muted by silent preparation or diminished by the sermon's delivery being diverted by an absorbing manuscript.

Nonetheless, when any preacher with whatever pulpit style proceeds by using the strategy of moving from *tension* to *resolution*, the power is much greater than if the sermon were to begin with homiletical resolution—followed with subsequent *therefores, oughts, shoulds,* and *musts.*

I am reminded of Frank Kermode's famous "tick-tock" analogy, and the almost electric power of the silence following the "tick," contrasted with what he called the "feeble apocalypse" of the silence following the "tock." (I remember as a child trying to reverse the tick and the tock of my grandmother's big mahogany clock on the mantle—but it seemed to need an act of God to accomplish the switch.)

For Paul Scott Wilson, the tension-to-resolution motif involves his understanding of the homiletical juxtaposition from Law to Gospel as the sermon's decisive shift. The plotted mobility of David Buttrick's system utilizes a similar shift from tension to resolution.

It was Haddon Robinson, the great traditional deductive preacher, who said that tension has to be introduced at the beginning of the introduction as well as with every point, and who then concluded by saying: "the moment you lose the tension, the sermon is over."[32] Is that why Frederick Buechner said: "The Gospel is bad news before it is good news"?[33]

Understand, I am not just talking about presentational style. Some have said about recent homiletical models: "Well, we have had a nice little intermission talking about sermon process and style; now it is time to get back to substance." Nonsense. We *are* talking about substance right here. If you want a thin sermon that is substantially bland, just never ask a question, never allow an issue to surface. Simply avoid tension; pile on a group of admonitions.

What maximizes the possibility of biblical/theological depth is pushing beneath simplistic affirmations and dull admonitions. Such textual exploration is the key to finding that tension/resolution matrix that cannot only engage the gospel but also the congregation. Said Begbie, the situation can be "sensed as directional, driving towards rest and closure. . . . We sense 'it is going somewhere.' "[34] The matter of narrative as strategic principle is not reducible to "presentational style." It moves toward ever increasing depth of engagement.

No wonder Fred Craddock warned preachers in his very first homiletical writing to not begin sermons with answers. In that first volume he used the terms *inductive* and *deductive,* noting that biblical exegesis is itself an inductive engagement. Although subsequent writings did not continue the language of induction, they continued to focus on the underlying principle, embodied by *expectancy, anticipation,* and *surprise.*

Craddock's concern for sermonic strategy was highlighted in his third volume, *Preaching,* by insisting that "it is difficult to overstate the vital role of anticipation in human life."[35] Turning to the one in the pulpit, he said, "The preacher understands the dynamic of anticipation, and therefore designs sermons which create expectation with their early promise, but which will delay the fulfillment of that promise until the listener is sufficiently engaged to own the message." Moreover: "All of this has one end in view: that hearer be moved to respond with attitudinal or behavioral change."[36]

Meanwhile, Walter Brueggemann speaks of the poet/ prophet who brings "a voice that shatters settled reality, and evokes new possibility in the listening assembly."[37] Please note the *tension-to-resolution* sequence in that last sentence ("shatters" to "evokes"). With wonderful angularity he continues, focusing on "speech . . . that destabilizes all our settled 'facts,' and opens the way for transformation and the gift of newness."[38] In fact, in his 1989 Lyman Beecher lectures, as printed in book form, even the chapter headings reflect the tension-resolution refrain:

"Numbness and Ache: The Strangeness of Healing"[39]
"Alienation and Rage: The Odd Invitation to Doxological Communion"[40]
"Restlessness and Greed: Obedience and Missional Imagination"[41]
"Resistance and Relinquishment: A Permit for Freedom"[42]

Indeed, tension and resolution are basic to music, glue for the novel, formulative for Aristotelian tragedy, and central to the movement of the sermon. I call it "moving from itch to scratch." But you need to be very careful about what you think I mean when I speak about "moving from itch to scratch." I am not talking about the itches with which people may be entering the sanctuary on a given Sunday morning. I am speaking about itches that are related to the text itself. That is why when teaching sermon preparation, I advise preachers to read aloud in numerous translations the text for the sermon. In the reading aloud I suggest they ask the question: "What is weird here? Not what's the point, because if first you ask about the point you will get 'home' before you want to—and the folks will go home before you want them to."

Indeed, in my first volume, *The Homiletical Plot*, I cited

Karl Barth, who noted "that we come to the Bible with our questions, and find only our own reflection."[43] The Bible must respond, "Nein, wrong question." I also cited Paul Scherer, who once said to not meet the listeners where they are because often they are "in the wrong place."[44] In short, the needed tension needs to emerge from the biblical text itself—in one form or another.

There is yet more to narrative strategy than the tension-resolution motif, in its numerous forms. H. Grady Davis refers to the kind of idea that is fermenting ideas with expanding force—often the kind of language that doesn't just sit there motionless on a page or a tongue. This I call:

The Narrative Strategy of Causative/Evocative/ Provocative Language

Instead of the evolutional accumulative nature of discursive language, it is the revolutional wholistic nature of what Langer called "presentational" language that is key here. Some would refer to it as a kind of aesthetic language that presents a gestaltive cognitive knowing—(not reducible to affect). This is the form of language that, as Sallie McFague puts it, uses words that "mean more than they ordinarily do"—that shuffles the deck, involving a metaphoric tease.[45]

Fred Craddock does it so smoothly that we hardly know what has hit us until it is too late to draw back. It gets in deeper than the ears. He calls it "triggering the mind," using language in which "the goal is not to utter but to evoke."[46] Unsurprisingly, he appeals to the five senses: "The weight of a grudge, the touch of friendship . . . , the taste of remorse,"[47] and so on. Such language does something with what it is talking about.

Gabriele Rico reminds us that F. Scott Fitzgerald, in *The Great Gatsby,* rather than utilizing ordinary language to explain just how wealthy Daisy is, simply said, "Her voice is full of money."[48] And that is not "indirect language" nor is it a bit of extra fluff. It evokes what it says. It is incarnated, embodied rather than abstracted language. One might speak here of *real presence.* It takes over. It does something.

So Walter Brueggemann calls out his hope for us in his Lyman Beecher Lectures of 1989, published as: *Finally Comes the Poet: Daring Speech for Proclamation.* He is not speaking particularly about rhythm or rhyme. By prose he means the kind of language that can be described as flat, "settled formulae" speech that causes "love letters [to] sound like memos." By poetic speech he means the kind of language that "moves like Bob Gibson's fastball, that jumps at the right moment"[49]

Clearly, what we need are linguistic poets in the pulpit. In fact one of the first that comes to mind is Leander Keck. Prior to becoming academic dean at Yale Divinity School (from which he is now retired), he taught New Testament at Candler School of Theology. On one particular occasion he was the preacher in the chapel service. The title of his sermon was "Limited Resources, Unlimited Possibilities." (Do you notice the tension/resolution motif here in his title?) His text focused on the Markan account of the feeding of the multitude. His opening line: "At one time or another, all of us have wondered, just what am I doing here?"[50] You know, that "itch" just might get the attention of a chapel full of M.Div. students. Once early in the sermon he described the Israelite reconnaissance into Caanan in the time of Moses. Said Keck, "You recall that the spies returned not simply with tales on their lips about the milk and honey, but also with terror in their hearts because there were giants in the land."[51] (By reading this last sentence aloud, you will be assisted in noticing the double parallel flow of the lines.) "Tales on their lips . . . terror in their hearts." That kind of speech will keep folks listening in chapel.

He finally got to the biblical text—with students probably wondering why it hadn't come sooner. He knew why. Preceding the text he whetted their appetite: "Strangely, it's a story whose point a prosaic mind can miss. In fact, on one level it's completely unbelievable; on another level, it can . . . but why spoil the story in advance?"[52] Finally, he moves to the text, and in its treatment he had occasion to mention sheep in their context: "nibbling their way into danger and death, baa-baaing their fears into the night."[53] One cannot but notice the power of those verbs at work.

Buechner's use of language is equally powerful. Recall his description of Pilate coming to his office to confront Jesus and to consider the charges against him. Perhaps you recall Buechner's image that Pilate was trying to quit smoking—and Buechner drew word-pictures about it. Moreover, Buechner could have taken quite a bit of time explaining the fundamental disconnect between Pilate and those he ruled. He didn't explain. No, he simply put Pilate in a limousine with tinted glass.[54]

Buechner also describes the kind of language use for which he is famous. "Words," he says, are not just understood, but are "image and symbol as well as meaning, are sound and rhythm, maybe above all are passion. . . . They set echoes going the way a choir in a great cathedral does, only it is we who become the cathedral and in us that the words echo."[55]

Did you notice that he actually does it while describing it? And then Tom Long comes by with a similar capacity. Note, for example: "Holy sounding talk with all the edges filed away."[56]

Barbara Brown Taylor's sermon on the Samaritan woman at the well is so powerful that *The Christian Century* has featured its manuscript in its publication twice in twelve years. In that sermon Taylor, after noting that Jesus talks longer with the Samaritan woman than with any other person in the Gospel accounts (I had never noticed that), suggested that was a peculiar choice because she was an outsider: "I mean outsider, and not only a woman, but a fallen woman, with as many husbands as Elizabeth Taylor."

And now observe how she then describes their meeting:

> When he lifts his head & asks her for a drink, she sees the olive skin, the dark eyes, the strong nose. He is no half-breed. This man is a Jew, but what in the world is he doing there? Has he lost his way? Has he lost his faith, to be talking to her like that?

It is worth noting here that Taylor does not go into discursive exploration about how deep is the question about why Jesus would even be there—given the relations between Jews and Samaritans. No, she doesn't want to handle it that way. Instead, she asks: "Has he lost his faith?" That's how radical this scene is. Then, after the conversational part about the woman's husbands, the woman thinks Jesus is getting too personal and switches the conversation back to the "safer" topic of religion. "But it does not work," Barbara Brown Taylor notices. "When she steps back, he steps toward her. When she steps out of the light, he steps into it. He will not let her retreat."[57]

Oh, my, that's called imagination. But note the kind. These images are not affective frills, not additional ideas, but the language of embodiment. Of course, one might respond, "Of course it is easy for people like Keck and Buechner and Taylor. But who of us are in their league?" Perhaps so, but all of us can be better—if in fact we understand the nature of strategic language. It is not beyond our grasp. It is within our work. Just don't give stale memos, like reports of last month's minutes. Linger. Imagine the scene. Utilize words that work. It is not a matter of adding peripheral detail; for Taylor it was more a matter of setting the stage for the woman's shock. She wants us to get inside that scene and imagine what it must have been like for the woman to be confronted by this Jew in Samaritan land. Rather than explanation she provided a visual moment. "She sees the olive skin. . . . He is no half-breed." Finding a powerful moment of tension within the text is far more likely to happen when one lingers to savor the flavor of a text. A large part of our difficulty is in knowing too well the text—skipping over what we have heard before, and hence becoming too certain of its meaning. Pausing in uncertainty can often be a powerfully creative moment in really hearing a text. Linger, listen, explore. Then when we come up with a curious possibility, we can pursue it further.

Another means of strategy is to reach further into Brueggemann's fundamental principle about the method and goal in the sermonic operation. Basically, he said instruction will not get it done. "If the text is to claim authority," he advised in his Yale lectures, "it will require neither the close reasoning of a canon lawyer, nor the precision of a technician, but it will require an artist to render the text in quite fresh ways, so that the text breaks life open among the baptized as it never has before."[58]

So, for example, Barbara Brown Taylor noticed not a simple difference, but a tension in the conversation between Jesus and the woman. She did not announce it or explain its cause. She put the image of light within it. So "when she steps back, he steps toward her. When she steps out of the light he steps into it."[59] Again, this is no frill; this is *embodying* what is going on. Joseph Sittler made clear in his Lyman Beecher Lecture of 1959 that the work of imagination is not cosmetical or decorative. "Imagination . . . is never an addition, it is an evocation."[60]

We have now considered Narrative as Temporal Modality— the sheer facticity of the sermonic event in time. We have engaged the matter of Narrative as Strategic Aim—the question of how best to utilize that time. Now we turn to the particulars of sermonic plot, the actual homiletic designs, the optimal range of ordered forms of moving time.

Level Three: Narrative as Embodied Form

My first model of *The Homiletical Plot* was published in the book of that title in 1980. Theoretically, the plot consisted of five stages: oops, ugh, aha, whee, and yeah. More descriptively, those five stages of the plot moved from (1) Upsetting the equilibrium, through (2) Analyzing the discrepancy, toward (3) Disclosing the clue to resolution, to (4) Experiencing the gospel, to finally (5) Anticipating the consequences.[61] It looked like this:

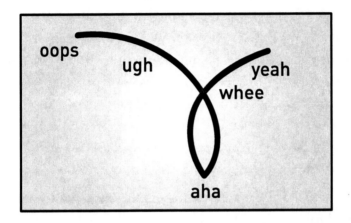

That was the last time I said it exactly that way. Since then it has been altered, nuanced, and enlarged, though never abandoned. These alterations have resulted from shifts both in my preaching modality and in light of differing textual homiletical needs.

Then, having discovered earlier that what has sometimes been called "left brain" thinking is not the only form of serious thought, I began to be more intentional about including this other (nondiscursive) form of thinking within my homiletical model. Hence, I began speaking of the second stage of the plot in differing terms. Hence, in my next writing, *Doing Time in the Pulpit* (1985), rather than using the term *analyzing*, I spoke of escalating, or indicated that the plot "thickens," that there is

31

a "swelling of suspense."[62] *Analyzing* was too limiting a term. Indeed, there are many ways of complicating the plot; analysis is only one.

Regarding step 3, disclosing the clue to resolution, I realized that the decisive turn is not always an absolute reversal. As a result I began to speak of the sudden shift or the "surprising turn."[63] The diagram shows the radical shift graphically noted by the sheerness of the point at the bottom. It may not always be an exact 180 degrees, but it is never a gradually sweeping turn. It is quickly decisive. In hindsight I recall that long before I ever spoke of "reversal" I drew the plotline with that angular point at the bottom of the drawing. (Michael Polanyi once said that sometimes "we know more than we can tell.")[64]

Likewise, I found that sometimes, such as the story of Bartimaeus, the good news of his healing (step 4) happens just prior to the reversal (step 3) instead of just after (with Jesus telling him to "go," but he choosing rather to "stay with Jesus.") Hence, sometimes the plotline runs 1, 2, 3, 4, 5; other times 1, 2, 4, 3, 5. Occasionally, as with Matthew's parable of the talents, steps 3 and 4 (the clue to resolution and experiencing the gospel) are virtually synonymous, or coterminous with the gospel *being* the decisive shift. (You recall that in that parable, the story begins with the owner having all the power. And the slaves know all about vulnerability. Then the owner delivers his assets to the slaves and leaves for an unspecified time. Now the slaves have the power and the owner has enormous vulnerability. The world is turned upside down. If they waste or lose his resources, he has no future. The decisive turn and the good news happen all at once.) This nuance of the plot was described in *The Sermon: Dancing the Edge of Mystery* in 1997 (Eugene Lowry; Abingdon Press).

Note that in all the various versions of the plot, there are still five steps or stages, but how the third and the fourth relate is varied either by the movement of the text or the homiletical purpose of the sermon. The following diagram is the latest version of the plot, with stage 4 (*whee*—good news) occurring just before, just after, or precisely at the sudden turn of the sermon. As pictured in the expanded edition of *The Homiletical Plot, Expanded Edition:*[65]

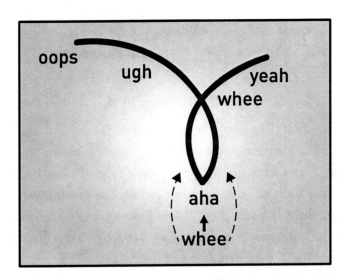

The crucial visual clues here involve noticing that the thought grows deeper into greater perplexity for more than half of the length of the sermon; the sudden shift or reversal of the sermon is way beyond midpoint, timewise. Likewise, the sudden shift or reversal is not a nice, smooth turn, but a startlingly sharp angular shift. (This principle of reversal was articulated by Aristotle long before.)

Notice also that I changed the name of the last stage from "consequences" to Aristotle's "denouement" or "unfolding." (My childhood experiences should have warned me about the negative connotation of the term *consequences*.) After all, the concluding stage or moment of the sermon—one way or another—is to anticipate the future, made new by the good news of the gospel.

So there are still five stages in the homiletical plot, but they are nuanced differently by the nature of the text, an enlarged understanding of the techniques of plot escalation (including image and story), the pastor's exegesis of the local congregation and world, and the sermonic purpose of the message.

Moving to the Future

The time has now come to explicitly name a further option in narrative preaching, another plotting mode. When, for example, one compares the type of plots used in television programming in 1980 (when *The Homiletical Plot* was published) with the kind of television plots currently employed, the matter of increasing narrative variety becomes illumined. In that first book, I used several TV plots for assistance in helping preachers grasp how plots work. But now, we have moved from watching *Columbo* on television and experiencing *High Noon* at the theater, to watching *NCIS* on television and seeing *Avatar* at the theater. Instead of Quincy the pathologist, we have *Grey's Anatomy,* instead of *Perry Mason* we have *Boston Legal.* (In greater detail I have explored several of these differences in another recently published writing.)[66] The shift in television reflects a shift in current practices of communication. By analogy the differences are quite telling regarding the art of preaching. And indeed, some current practices of narrative preaching already reflect these changes. Yet perhaps this form has not yet been named broadly in the kind of comprehensive way that can maximize its use.

Episodal Narrative Form

The term *episodal preaching* reflects a newly named way to imagine how biblical/sermonic ideas can move from opening disequilibrium to concluding resolution—but in a different kind of move from "oops" to "yeah." The term *episodal* suggests a different means of facilitating that "itch" to "scratch" event in time called the sermon.

On several occasions I have told Tom Troeger that he is perfectly situated to focus on what I am calling episodal preaching because, indeed, he practices it often. Below I will share one of his sermon manuscripts that operates in precisely this kind of narrative mode. He published it over twenty years ago in his book, *Imagining a Sermon.*[67] I have said that there is very little literature based on this often-used method, but now I will have to modify that statement. Perhaps the issue is in part one of nomenclature.

For example, I have often spoken of David Buttrick's method of plotted mobility for preaching simply as a more stringently structured form of my kind of narrative preaching. Indeed, on several occasions I have followed carefully the manuscripts of several of his sermons, and compared them with my treatment of the same biblical texts. In one such perusal of his manuscript, I wrote: *oops, ugh, aha, whee,* and *yeah* in the margins that occur in precisely the same order as my sermon on that text. Clearly, both of us move in strikingly similar ways.

Yet the five or six "moves" in his sermonic system are deliberately planned with openings and closings for each of the individual moves. This is a critical difference in form from my connectional transitional shifts—from *oops* to *ugh,* and so on. Clearly his linearity of movement is different from mine. One way to describe this particular difference in how he plots the sermon's movement—as contrasted with my plot process—can be captured accurately, I believe, by the term *episodal.* After all, each Buttrick move represents a kind of self-contained identifiable episode. It is still moving in a time sequence, and still delaying the final resolution that happens in the various kinds of narrative preaching, but the plotted mobility happens differently.

All of which is to say that to think this way is also to note that indeed we are not without considerable literature on the subject of episodal preaching! Buttrick has been encouraging us this way for decades now. I suggest that his important work—both articulate and embodied—might be summarized accurately by the term *vertically plotted mobility.*

Perhaps noting two kinds of jazz improvisation may be helpful here—even for those who would claim no knowledge whatever about jazz. In simple terms one might say that most jazz improvisation works dominantly either horizontally or vertically. What I am describing here is something that you probably already know but don't know you know because you have never heard the terms just now used. But you probably have noticed that some of us who play jazz improvise with the focus on the tune's melody line throughout the performance, that is, work more traditionally, more horizontally. Other, more "progressive" style musicians improvise with a greater focus on the harmonic structure.

That is, in the first case the musicians never get too far away from the melody. Snatches of it come frequently, and listeners continue knowing what song is being played. On the other hand, more "sophisticated" jazz musicians (after the likes of Parker and Coltrane), after the first chorus rendering of the melody, begin playing vertical flourishes around the chord structure movements. So if you have heard a whole chorus of a jazz number played without your ever hearing the melody line, likely you were listening to "progressive" jazz by those who work sequentially up and down the harmonic floor—that is, in forward-moving vertical episodes.

Also, you might have noticed that the soloist never begins the riff on beat number one. Others strike the chord or give the beat, and then the soloist runs up and down and around the harmonics. This is vertical improvisation. Understand, the music is still moving forward, going somewhere, but the musicians may not tell you where until quite a while later. Generally, progressive musicians will finally return to a concluding melody chorus to complete the presentation. So the vertical improvisation is set within beginning and ending brackets of traditional horizontal jazz that clarify the song being played. And it should be noticed that quite a number of fine jazz artists blend both horizontal and vertically based moves in their improvised performance of a song. But identifying the difference in either-or terms, while somewhat simplistic, is helpful for clarity.

Where I am heading with this brief musical interlude is to say that I preach horizontally, working in and around the ongoing text and theme. Buttrick more often provides a "self-contained" vertical episode series. Those five or six episodes also move forward with the ongoing text and theme but involve more separable vignettes along the way. His narrativity moves forward by means of episodal (or vertical) blocks. Buttrick and I may come out quite similarly by the time the sermon is concluded. Yet our routes are somewhat differently shaped.

Then there is Craddock's method of preaching, once called *inductive*, later identified as illustrating a particular form of preaching he called *narrative*, and more recently understood simply as utilizing the principle of *expectancy and surprise*—the increase of anticipation, together with a strategic delay of sermonic resolution. Craddock typically begins by leading the congregation into an exploration of a biblical text. We follow him into significant textual examination not yet complete, when, all of a sudden, he leaves the text. He never warns us. He never signals before turning. Without transition, we suddenly find ourselves in aisle eleven of the supermarket we've been going to for ten years now. One might ask, "Well, how did we get there?" More than likely we will simply trust Fred to take us where he wants. He's done it with us before, you know. The fascinating thing about the eleventh aisle of the supermarket—and what we remember of similar shifts of focus in other texts and sermons—is that Fred Craddock is going to spot something there in aisle eleven that we have never noticed for the entire ten years we have been walking through it. He will spot something crucial to the matter at hand and name it. While we are wondering how we missed something that important—and are amazed by how it is that he managed to spot it—he is busy jumping nicely into yet another text. By this time we are caught up in ever-escalating anticipation and know clearly that he will lead us to the gospel—when, in fact, it is time. That is the way he works, and it is clearly episodal in form. The quick moves from one context to another might be seen as a kind of vertical jump. Yet, while we may not yet know, it is indeed moving us forward toward the overall sermonic resolution.

Note the clear difference from my more horizontal plotting movement. I too begin with exploration of a biblical text. Then toward the next movement of the sermonic plot I look for a "thin thread transition." (Note that I did not say "thin thought transition.") Hopefully, this kind of transition will lure the congregation from one sequence position of the plotline into the next. Perhaps a symphony concert moment will assist in making clear what I mean.

There was a surprising musical transition that occurred in a particular concert I once attended. I do not now even remember the composition nor the place—let alone the key they were in. But what I do remember is when the orchestra concluded the first section or movement of the musical score with a decisive sweep of the conductor's baton, I expected the customary momentary silence that would happen between movements. But instead, there was one instrument still playing. It was an oboe, cutting into the silence—and it was not a mistake being made. The oboe was providing the kind of thin, sharp line between the sections of music that only an oboe can accomplish. The oboist's note was the fifth of the root of the section just concluded—and also the third of the new harmonic root that would follow. (Such as the note G, which is the fifth position in the key of C, which then is immediately transformed into the third position in the key of E♭.)

This is precisely the kind of transitional turn that I recommend for preachers when moving from one section of a sermon to the next. My concern is that one ought never expect that a congregation will be able to move from one mountain of material to another mountain of material in one huge leap. Find a thin but certain connection, that—to mix the metaphor—will provide the glue of transition.

For example, in the Lukan account of Simon's call, when the fishing boats are filled incredibly high with fish, Simon says to Jesus: "Go away!" Unbelievable. Why would he say that at this wonderful moment? One needs to explore this unsettling demand further. Does it feel like a twilight-zone cry, perhaps, born of the mystery of it all? "Go away"? But this is no time for a "left brain" exploration into the experience of the Holy, such as saying to the congregation: "Perhaps this is a good time to consider the nature of the unusual experience of mystery." That is exactly what I want to do, but such a transition is likely too thick for folks to traverse. My alternative is to say something more like: "This is not the first time in Scripture that such a reaction has occurred. Remember Isaiah when he had his vision of the Lord high and lifted up?"

This is what I mean by a "thin line" to link last to next. Once inside Isaiah 6, greater exploration can evolve. But first, one needs to jump quickly into Isaiah's dramatic vision of "the Lord . . . high and lofty," so that he can help us picture the moment and hence lead our exploration.[68]

Obviously, however, Fred does not need my suggestion because when he makes a move, we all make the move together. In fact, often those preachers who work more episodically sometimes make transitions that are more implicit than explicit. I believe that this is a strategy much more difficult and risky, but it can be done by some.

Tom Troeger is another who can do it wonderfully. And he is the one I believe can help us further understand the way episodical forms of narrative preaching might work. In his *Imagining a Sermon*, back in 1990, he tells a true story of being called to be the wedding liturgist for a couple getting married. (It is important to note that this event happened just previous to the publication of his book.)

He called his first version of the wedding sermon preparation process an attempt to provide "a sample rhetorical sermon for the print generation." I knew he was speaking of people in my generation. He said, "I turn on the word processor," and he begins his first attempt to frame the sermon. You will note its traditional sermonic format.

> In a few moments Catherine and Jonathan will repeat their vows, "I promise and covenant before God and these witnesses to be your faithful and loving wife/husband for better for worse, for richer for poorer, in sickness and in health as long as we both shall live."

Promise and *covenant*—what antique words they are to our ears. They sound like something we might find carved in Romanesque letters on a stone monument. . . .

Promise and *covenant*—they are not the words of everyday speech. They are not the words we use during coffee break or on the street. . . .

Promise and *covenant*—these are sacred words [that] set loose once again the voices of Abraham and Sarah; Moses and the prophets; the apostles and the martyrs.

They remind us that God has made a promise to us; to guide us, to support us, to love us, to hold us to account for how we live. And we have made a promise to God: to be faithful, to do justice, to show compassion, to witness to our faith in Jesus Christ.

Promise and *covenant*, these are words that are deeper than feeling. . . . Feelings alone are an inadequate foundation for a marriage. . . .

Promise and *covenant* do not change with our moods. When we promise and covenant, we make a commitment, a pledge, to be faithful partners to each other no matter what happens—for better for worse, for richer for poorer, in sickness and in health. . . .

Remember [these words] in the night when a child cries.

Remember them when bitter speech has passed between you.

Remember them when your bodies fail from illness or age.

Remember that you spoke these words to each other.

In the remembering hear again the voice of One who loves you with an everlasting love and who will supply the grace and strength to keep the promise and covenant that you are making this day.[69]

Well, Troeger did not particularly like it. He didn't put it that way, but that was clear because he chose something else. He decided to prepare a sermon for this wedding that he calls "a sample visual sermon for the mass media generation." Notice that the "visual" mode is not something projected onto a screen. It is prompted inside listeners' minds by spoken images:

> I once met a couple who told me that every anniversary they donned their wedding clothes and had their picture taken in the living room of their house. They planned to do it throughout their life together and to collect the photographs in a single album.
>
> As you, Catherine and Jonathan, stand before this congregation in your wedding clothes, I am remembering that other couple. I imagine them on their fifth anniversary, coming down to the living room for their annual picture. She is in her white gown, and he is wearing his three-piece suit. . . . They are waiting for their next door neighbor who has gone to get some extra flashcubes.
>
> The first four years, they hired a professional photographer, but this has not been a good year. . . . The husband lost his job. The wife is only able to get part-time employment, and their second child is having medical problems.
>
> Finally, their neighbor arrives. He positions them in front of the fireplace and suggests they hold hands . . . the way you, Catherine and Jonathan, will do in a few minutes when you say [your vows].
>
> While their friend fidgets with the focus, the wife notices the stuffing that is coming out of the sofa and wishes they had money to redo it. . . .
>
> Flash! "That's picture number one," says their friend.
>
> . . . The wife says to her husband, "Do you remember our vows? We memorized them."
>
> They think a moment, then slowly repeat together, "I promise and covenant before God and these witnesses to be your faithful and loving wife/husband for better for worse, for richer for poorer. . . ."

Poorer. The word bursts like the flashcube on their friend's camera and highlights the stack of bills on the table beneath the phone and the calendar marked with doctor's appointments they cannot afford. A look leaps between them.

"We promised."

The camera flashes again.

"That will be a good one," exclaims their friend.

Next I picture the couple ten years later. Things are much better for them financially. The husband has a good job. The wife went back to school and has just taken an excellent position. . . . Each of the children has a ten-speed bicycle in the garage.

But the husband and wife have thrown acid words at each other. The second child, after all those trips to the doctor, is in trouble. Each partner has said to the other: "If you were not so preoccupied with your job and could give some time to the family, then things would be different."

On their fifteenth anniversary they come home and say they are too tired to get into the old wedding clothes. Then they remember that the photographer is coming in twenty minutes and has probably already left her studio and will charge them for the visit no matter what. So they trek up to the attic and throw themselves into the musty clothes, discovering that they have to suck in to get the zippers shut.

The doorbell rings.

The photographer comes in and takes control. "Come on now. Hold hands. A smile for the camera."

While the photographer clicks away they get lost in the moment and begin to repeat the vow: "I do promise and covenant before God and these witnesses to be your loving and faithful wife/husband for better for worse. . . ."

Worse flashes as brightly as *poorer* did ten years before, and again the look leaps between them: "We promised."

Finally I picture their forty-seventh anniversary. They do

not know whether they'll make it to their fiftieth. He has had two heart attacks, and her hands are crooked with arthritis. Their granddaughter, herself engaged, is upstairs bringing down the old clothes. The dress has yellowed, and when the wife puts it on she tears a seam. The husband cannot get the trousers zippered, but if the picture is taken from the waist up and he buttons the coat, it will be all right.

He takes his wife's hands, her knuckles swollen and knobby, and out of their faltering bodies arises in a whisper the sacred pledge: "I do covenant before God and these witnesses to be your faithful and loving wife/husband for better for worse, for richer for poorer, in sickness and in health until death do us part."

In sickness . . . until death. . . . Words that had slipped easily out of their mouths on their wedding day are now heavy with meaning.

"I've got to go upstairs to get more film," says the granddaughter.

But they are not listening. In looking into each other's eyes, they see something more beautiful than the prize pictures in their anniversary album: the grace and the glory of a promise kept.

That is our prayer for you, Catherine and Jonathan, that for better for worse, for richer for poorer, in sickness and in health, until death do you part, that you may know the grace and the glory of a promise kept. May God, who has made an everlasting covenant with us, grant you the strength to keep your covenant for a lifetime.[70]

What a transformation! Of course, one might claim that we have the same theological/homiletical content involved in both versions. Yet such an observation would not be taking into consideration the remarkable transformation of power that the shift of form from didactic to episodal has accomplished.

The transitional glue in the episodal form is that recurring thin line of movement facilitated by "annual pictures for a scrapbook." One may again recall Fred Craddock's remark that the homiletical goal is not about getting something said, but getting something heard.[71]

It is my hope that by naming and illustrating this particular kind of plotted or narrative preaching as *episodal,* preachers may not only begin to sense the variety of homiletic possibilities but, indeed, become able to implement increasing varieties. It is often the case that those of us who both teach and write will have some students or readers respond to our work by saying not so much that they learned things altogether new about preaching as much as that they were given names and handles for their own practice of preaching. Hopefully, such handles migrate into preachers' own newly developed norms and goals.

Utterly crucial is H. Grady Davis's conviction that if we are to learn from other arts they must be those arts that involve time sequence. Sometimes our reflections about our own avocational hobbies and interests can prompt narrative realities that can be quite useful in our understanding of the role of preaching. Whether cooking in the kitchen or carving in the workshop, considering the narrative stages of those other activities can be powerful learning tools for preaching.

Following Davis's lead, our next agenda is to blend Aristotle's take on plot with the live experience of music, particularly jazz, as a way to better understand our call to preach.

Chapter 3, "Encountering the Aristotle Blues," combines Aristotle's understanding of plot, together with jazz improvisation's method of working, and applies them to selected scriptural passages. At Yale and at McAfee this became a musical-homiletic experience. At Yale I was joined by Mac McCune on trumpet and Carlos Summers on trombone. The reader may experience this recorded live event online; see the link at the beginning of chapter 3.

ENCOUNTERING THE ARISTOTLE BLUES[1]

For the fullest experience of this chapter, hear the accompanying recording at http://www.abingdonpress.com/the-homiletical-beat/, or connect by means of the QR (quick response) symbol.

In chapter 2 I grounded my work by noting the profound observation of H. Grady Davis, who said, "If we wish to learn from other arts, we must learn from these arts based on a time sequence."[2] With the assistance of Aristotle, I now hope to do precisely that.

I moved from debate hall to pulpit as a sophomore in college when I was appointed by a Methodist bishop to serve a "student charge." I was paid to practice on those poor people who had to endure my first attempts to preach. I continued my attempts through seminary as well—and did about the same thing.

It was deductive; it was argumentative; it pushed toward a conclusion. My mother, who was present for my first sermon, expressed her appreciation. "It was lovely, Eugene," she said. Later, however, she added, "it did sound like a debate."

It is strange that this should be true, because of my experience with jazz. I started playing the piano prior to kindergarten to get back at my older brother, who after finishing piano practice would close the Thompson primer. I then would move to the piano and play by ear what he had been attempting to play with the help of the Thompson book. This just irritated the devil out of him—to my delight. Soon my parents decided that I, too, should begin taking piano lessons. I was five at the time. By seventh grade I was playing piano in a jazz band run by a high school student. Throughout high school I ran my own stock dance band. I also played trombone in a blues band. In college, I formed another band, The Blue Notes—until my District Board of Ministry decided that running a dance band was not suitable for one appointed pastor of a local congregation.

Now, many years later, I just wish that somebody had said to me, "When you are preparing to preach, remember to preach the same way you play the piano." I would have understood the narrative principle of preaching years more quickly than I did. Early on I learned that for jazz improvisation, you take a simple tune and by "messing around with the melody and the harmony" you turn the song sideways. It becomes more complicated, more interesting, and finally turns toward the reprise called home.

My early argumentative and deductive approach to preaching was not helped much in seminary courses in preaching that I took at Drew. The textbook was *Principles and Practices of Preaching*, by Ilion T. Jones. His view was that after some idea "strikes," the preparation process begins with three steps. First, one works on the idea until it becomes quite crisp—he calls it "the exact truth the idea contains." Second, one figures out what to do with that idea. Jones wanted clarity about the intended sermonic "purpose." "State clearly in a brief sentence . . . the purpose of the sermon." Step three: "Find a suitable passage from the Bible on which to base the sermon."[3]

I really didn't need to heed that advice at that time in my sermon work. Unfortunately, that's what I already had been doing as a college-student preacher.

Within ten years, I finally began to understand something about the notion of narrativity in preaching. Yet it was still logical; it was still discursive; it was still "pushy." But then I began to find wider reaches of mood and purpose. It was then that I wrote *Doing Time in the Pulpit*—as I was beginning to grasp the difference between space and time. As I noted, a sermon is not an object in space, it is an event in time. It moves like music moves. It starts with a beginning and stops at the end. That's how it works—beat after beat.

A simple scale on the piano illustrates the growing thickness and final resolution as it moves slowly from middle C upward through the entire octave. The timing is crucial. If you reach the resolution of the high C too soon, you will have killed it.

Don't forget Jeremy Begbie and the twin elements of tension and resolution in music.

It was Aristotle whose understanding of plot assisted me in first naming *plot* as basic to every sermon of whatever type.[4] And it was Aristotle whose grasp of the stages of the classic plot lured me away from the dominance of narrow discursive ideation. Now, encountering the Aristotle Blues can help us all better understand those stages.

Stages of the Plot

Conflict

The sermon begins with something unsettling. Actually, often you do not have to have a large dose of conflict. Sometimes you only need to tweak it somehow—some small bit of surprise, something unexpected. For example, consider the classic hymn "Amazing Grace."

"Amazing Grace"

We've heard it the usual way many times. So what might a musician do to make it move differently—to catch the ear? One way is to change just one chord in the first phrase. Just one will do. The destination remains the same, but you simply get there by means of a different door—one not expected. Further changes to the chordal structure of the song will increase the tension and in turn the satisfaction when we finally walk it home.[5]

It reminds me of the two men on the road to Emmaus, found in Luke 24:13-35. One of the first things that needs to be asked is, what are they doing out there on the road? The text has already announced that a group of people including Mary, Jesus' mother; Peter; and others had made a couple of trips to the tomb. That group included "the eleven and . . . all the rest."[6] Now it says, "two of them were going to a village called Emmaus."[7]

Two "of *them*"?

What are *they* doing out there—when *their* group is huddled together somewhere close to the tomb? Some women had gone to the tomb, found the stone rolled away, and met two men in dazzling clothes who said Jesus had risen. The women reported all this to the whole group, who dismissed it as an idle tale. (This sometimes still happens.) Peter sprints back to the tomb to check for himself, but "two of them," Cleopas and his friend, are on a road headed, not to the tomb, but rather toward Emmaus. Why? Within the larger group, many are hugging each other in deep despair because their leader is gone forever. Others may be hugging in newfound hope that maybe death is not the last word after all.

Homiletically, to ask the question why, of all times, these two have separated themselves from their own group—out on any other road—is to prompt a journey most peculiar. It is made even more peculiar in that they do not even know their friend when he meets them on the road—which now is to be doubly separated. Once in Emmaus, and the guest invited to break the bread, he is known for who He is. And immediately, he disappears (surely a touch of divine humor), and quickly, within the hour, they head back to Jerusalem. One might call it a reversal.

We could feel sorry for them. Isn't it a shame! It's dark by now. Heading to Emmaus, they were walking in the light of day, but now, after the sun has set, they have to travel in the dark. Don't believe it. It was in the daytime while the sun was shining that they were walking in the dark. Now, with the sun long gone, they walk in the light! Asking the question of why they were out on the road to begin with is to tweak one's grasp of the story into a quite different trip. It is prompted simply by walking through a different door.

Sometimes there is more explicit conflict. For example, Paul Scott Wilson speaks of juxtaposition, the interface of disparate realities. Such a juxtaposition is captured by "Swinging Shepherd Blues."

"Swinging Shepherd Blues"

"Swinging Shepherd Blues" is a song that alternates between tension and resolution in almost every measure of the music's movement. Recall Begbie's image in chapter 2, with its overlapping episodes of tension-resolution. Just when a dissonant chord moves to clear harmony in the next beat or measure and we think we are free of trouble, the music jumps into yet another form of conflict. Both the song and the parable complete the tension-resolution modality repeatedly in quick succession.

What the world calls the "prodigal son" story illustrates this modality.

"You know, Dad, we love you, and we know that some day you will die. But I have a life to live, and I'm not planning on doing it here. So do you suppose that we could just pretend that you've already died?" And so the father divides his substance between his two sons.

The younger son heads off to the far country and has a grand time. "This round's on me," he exclaims. But then a famine strikes, and the money runs out. So do his friends. Not like back at home. He has to find a place to land, and he does—hiring out to feed pigs in a gentile farmer's farm. He gets a swine's eye view of life. He would like to eat what the pigs are eating, but no one gives him anything.

Finally, he comes to himself (note the phrase). Helmut Thielicke once observed that the son didn't get so sick of the pigpen that he turned home. It was his understanding of home that made him so sick of the pigpen.[8] He heads home, memorizing his confession; but his father runs down the lane and his confession gets interrupted by a hug, a robe, a ring, and a pair of sandals. It's party time.

As Begbie notes, there are teleological principles involved here. It has direction. We sense it is going somewhere—actually both the text and the song. Obviously there are lots of differing ways for songs to go somewhere.

David Schlafer has noted at least three differing homiletical modalities that are possible in carrying the sermon's freight of thought through the process of the plot. They are *logic, image,* or *story.*[9] When preaching on the Twenty-third Psalm images may easily carry the freight of thought. With a parable of Jesus, listeners probably expect the preacher will somehow run the parable in expanded story form. If Paul's argument with the Galatians is being handled, logic will likely be key. (Understand, one modality will be central; the other two more peripheral.) Conflict, dissonance, complication, and surprise of reversal— they are all involved in the shape of the presentation, but function differently depending on the mode of the presentation that best fits the text and the sermonic purpose.

But alas, preachers often make a major strategic mistake. Their eagerness to arrive at their homiletical destination lures them toward final resolution way too soon—without fully escalating the opening tension. Just now, the preacher needs to enable greater struggle with the text's central issue. (One might notice how anxious some preachers become to quickly "get to Jesus.") Ah, closure does feel so good. If we don't watch it, though, we may slip into pale resolution, and arrive home way too soon, and so might they. As Craddock has instructed us, delaying fulfillment is the key at this point.

Unfortunately, often it is a touch of admonition that supplants this crucial strategy of delaying fulfillment. For example, any naming of some current Christian failing can put the sermon to sleep by immediately reminding the congregation to become more fully committed in their discipleship. Once that happens, the sermon falls into an ethic of obedience that is about as powerful as most New Year's resolutions: "Yes, let us do better." But that means no gospel of Christ here, no empowerment here, just good advice. The purpose of delaying fulfillment is to allow the handling of the text to probe the issue deeply enough that the power of the gospel can be proclaimed. Hence, what is needed now is . . .

Complication

"On the Sunny Side of the Street"

Something is needed to exacerbate the issue at stake. The song "On the Sunny Side of the Street" may assist us here. Many artists have missed the real issue lying underneath the listening experience. The sheet music tells the musician how to play or sing the song. It advises "*Giocoso*," which means "merrily, lively, playfully." All of which mises the song altogether. Such advise is wrong.

Why would anyone call for a "playful" rendering? Perhaps the mistake might have emerged because of the sad previous verse (often missing in the sheet music) that tells a tale of loneliness being intercepted wonderfully by amorous connection.

But the tension to resolution motif in this musical text has little to do with the move from loneliness to love. The real torque comes from the historical context, that terrible moment in time when the song was composed. Dorothy Fields wrote the song in the midst of the Great Depression—within the year of the fall of the Wall Street banks.

The powerful, poignant moment in the song arrives when it says, "If I never have a cent"—which was certainly a possibility in 1930.

"If I never have a cent, I'll be rich as Rockefeller. Gold dust at my feet, on the sunny side of the street."

Here is a song attempting to make some kind of good news possible in the most desperate moments of the Great Depression. The music as performed must reveal this touch of hope in the midst of incredible pain—not *Giocoso*. (The blues understands this very well, very well, knowing that celebration seldom represents the absence of trouble.) So the powerful presentational torque here must connect the historical situation in which the song was composed to the human story set within it.[10]

It makes me think of Paul's Letter to the Philippians. Sections of that letter sound hopelessly optimistic. I don't believe there is any other letter of Paul that has so many "rejoices" in it. Over and over, not only speaking of his own rejoicing, but urging the church at Philippi to rejoice as well. Two verses have two "rejoices" in the same sentence! In the third chapter Paul declares, "One thing I do: forgetting what lies behind and straining forward to what lies ahead, I press on toward the goal for the prize of the heavenly call of God in Christ Jesus."[11] Well, Paul sounds like he is on a prosperity speaking tour. But he is not.

And when he speaks of straining forward, just how far forward is he likely to strain? Oh, perhaps eight feet or a little more. Then he will run smack into the bars of the jail cell. He is in prison, probably for his last time. We can hope the preacher who has chosen this text remembers chapters 1, 2, and the first part of chapter 3. Recall that Paul said that he didn't know which was better: to die and be with Christ or come back to be with them in Philippi. He concludes that his preference is to be with Christ, but it may be necessary to come back to them to share in "your progress and joy."[12] Apparently, he never made it back.

It is precisely in the context of his final imprisonment that Paul rejoices. How can he do that? Rejoice? Well, it is time in the sermon to recall verse 21 of the first chapter: "For to me, living is Christ and dying is gain."[13] Only *this* reality is enough to avoid absolute despair. Only because of Christ. No wonder he can talk about rejoicing. Indeed, Philippians 1:21 provides the gospel's resolution to the imprisonment's tension, *but the timing of the announcement is everything.*

If you miss the context, you have no torque. If you mention the imprisonment first, the power of reversal is sapped. Sequence is crucial. Buttrick spoke of how sometimes it is important in the sermon *not* to follow the chronology of the text.

Another way to complicate the musical plot is by chordal shock. The chorus of a song may begin with tight harmonic chords, slow movement, and quiet volume. But when the musician plays a strongly dissonant chord, the effect is jolting and stays that way until the next chorus returns for resolution. Once the shock happens, there is no way to return to the "old" chorus. It is now a new resolution because of what has happened in the meantime.

There is a passage in Exodus that works the same way— chapter 32, beginning with verse 6. Moses is up on the mountain. He and God are having a conversation. It is not a happy conversation. God says, "I am burning hot with anger. And *you,* who brought these people out of Egypt—these who now are acting perversely—*you,* you go down at once."[14] God is not through talking or pledging what he is going to do. "I have seen this people, how stiff-necked they are. Now let me alone, so that my wrath may burn hot against them and I may consume them."[15]

Moses responds to the anger and the command with: "O LORD, why does *your* wrath burn hot against *your* people, whom *you* brought out of the land of Egypt with great power and with a mighty hand?"[16] Moses suggests that God remember the promise and covenant God has already made with Abraham, and Isaac, and Israel, "*your* servants." In fact he details some of the particulars of God's promises. And indeed implores God to be true to who God is: "Turn from your fierce wrath; change your mind and do not bring disaster on your people."[17] Be true to yourself is Moses' central strategic pitch.

Once you discover in that conversation the absolute reversal of who's who and who's in charge of what, nothing is the same again—because of where we have been in the meantime. "And the LORD changed his mind about the disaster that he planned to bring on his people."[18] There is another way to increase the tension, the complication of a plot, and one may learn from the experience of it in musical form. The great jazz artist Cannonball Adderley made famous the song "Mercy, Mercy, Mercy."

"Mercy, Mercy, Mercy"

Although others have written several different lyrics for the tune, when Cannonball performs it, he uses none of them, except for the title. He allows the flow of music alone to get it said—although he did utilize words to begin the recording, prior to the music itself.

"You know," he began, "sometimes we are not prepared for adversity. Sometimes when it happens, we are caught short. Adversity takes over for all of us. I got it from my piano player who wrote this tune. It sounds like what you're supposed to say when you have that kind of problem. The words are, mercy,

mercy, mercy." Then the music begins. You will hear the cry—and perhaps you will hear something else besides that cry for mercy.

In several repeated moments in the song, there is actually no sound at all, just a full measure of silence, like those very long moments immediately after the call for mercy in our own lives. Those measures of silence are literally placed into the song repeatedly. Each time it happens, folks almost lean forward, waiting for the music to break the silence. The moments of silence are probably the most powerful parts of the song. The silence; the presence of that silence.

It is true. Sometimes all you can do is cry "mercy, mercy, mercy," and then wait—wait to see if there is a presence in the midst of the absence. George Buttrick in his 1931 Lyman Beecher lecture reminded us that the world will listen to the preacher who has "made friends with the silence in which God speaks."[19]

Another form of complication is revealed in musical experience when there are not only multiple meanings but even contradictory ones in the same song.

"His Eye Is on the Sparrow"

"His Eye Is on the Sparrow" involves just such a complication. The verse is quite sad. "Why should I feel discouraged" is one of four brief, short questions that are not rhetorical. Immediately it seems to imply that indeed one is discouraged. The short, almost staccato, musical phrase concurs. Short little blurbs they are.

"Why should the shadows come." Oh, it feels worse yet. "Why should my heart be lonely." Really. "And long for heaven and home." That's how bad it is. "When Jesus is my portion?" Did you notice the final phrase ends with a question mark? And "my constant friend is He" somehow does not bring certainty to the affirmation, "His eye is on the sparrow, and I know He watches me." Maybe. Sounds like it ought to be, but is it really? Notice how the phrases as heard limp along in their apparent uncertainty.

The song is not always played that way, but Mahalia Jackson's version is very clear about it.

But then here comes the chorus, in quick, rhythmic affirmation: "I sing because I'm happy; I sing because I'm free." Night to day. Clear, believable celebration. "For His eye is on the sparrow." Musically, this is a different world from the verse. "And I know He watches me." And the music has jumped from limping to dancing.

Isn't this wonderful? We have jumped from utter trouble into immeasurable joy. But hold on just a little bit. There are two more verses. They too are full of trouble. The second verse talks about doubts and fears. The third one is worse yet: "Whenever I am tempted, whenever clouds arise. When song gives place to sighing, when hope within me dies. I draw the closer to Him." When hope within me *dies*? Yes, but here comes the chorus again—with hope full-bore.

We are dealing here with repeated tension/resolution modalities—verse/chorus, trouble/grace. It is far deeper than plain contradiction. Note that the tension is still present within the celebration. This is not empty good time. There is an overcoming within the resolution. Oppressed peoples understand this better than some of the rest of us. This is the way the gospel works. And the jazz called "blues" plays it just right. The good news is in the midst of; exactly in the midst of. And this is not only how you complicate the plot. It also represents the decisive turn of the plot into resolution. It happens by means of the gospel.

Peripeteia

So it is that the plot is set for a reversal of movement, a sudden shift, a radical turn of some kind. Nicodemus in the presence of Jesus can help us understand how it might happen.

He came by night to see Jesus, surely past midnight. It is the story of Nic at Night. The first piece of the conversation did not go very well. He began the conversation by saying, "You must be the one, for no one could do what you do without the power of God." Jesus responds, "You can't get here from there."[20] It is an immediate disconnect. It is not a matter of adding up the score until arriving at faith.

In rebuke, Jesus utters a line that has been made famous by road signs even to this day. I didn't like them even as a child, looking out the window at western Kansas farmland from the backseat of an old car. "Ye must be born again,"[21] the amateurishly painted signs declared. Seemed a little pushy to me. Why don't they mind their own business, not try to mind mine? Just not friendly like the Burma Shave signs were.

So Jesus responds to Nicodemus by saying you must be born again, or from above or over again—depending on the translation. Poor Nic, I feel sorry for him. Nicodemus was not big on metaphor. He thought Jesus was talking gynecology. Then he gets a bit crude. He asks, "How can a grown man crawl back into his mother's womb?"[22] His question makes us wonder if this is not a clue about his motive in the midnight hour of his trip to see Jesus. His query is a form of the question: "What must I do, what is required, how can I get things right between me, God, and the world?" He is asking, "How do I do it? Crawl back?"

Jesus answers, "The wind blows where it wants; you don't know where it comes from or where it is headed, but you can feel it as it passes by."[23] Oh no, not Nic. He is too busy running in the night to find out what he must yet do. So the matter is not pushy, not demanding as I thought as a child. No, the matter has to do with an offer. What Jesus was saying to Nicodemus is that what you need you cannot provide. It is at least the one thing nobody can do. No matter how skilled, how wonderful, how talented, how virtuous one is, no one can birth oneself. It is always the gift of another.

Once you have said this in a sermon, there is no turning back, no way to rehash the opening disconnect. That part is gone. The offer is what is before us. Everything has now changed. The grace of it all is present. Whatever gets said now in the sermon is post-turn, post-clue, post-announcement. Even if you repeat something from earlier in the sermon, it is now utterly different.

In writing about the homiletical plot, I have noted that this reversal, this "aha" moment, the fundamental turning point in the sermon, is always related to the good news of the gospel. As I make clear in my later writings, the reversal is either just before the good news of the gospel is announced, just after the good news, or sometimes precisely the reversal point. That is why I have chosen to list the process in five moves—*conflict*, or upsetting of the equilibrium; *complication*, or escalation of the plot; the *reversal*, or *peripeteia*, that changes everything; the experience of the *gospel*; and finally the anticipation of the future, or *denouement*. In the case of Nicodemus, the reversal of the plot *is* precisely Jesus' announcement that to be born again is not an achievement at all, not a duty named, not a further demand, but rather a gift offered. No wonder listeners can never return to the opening conversation. Everything now has become new.

A hymnal can assist us to understand the process, and early forms of jazz can demonstrate. Many hymns, particularly the simpler ones, utilize an AABA format—major theme once, major theme again, shift to bridge theme, and back to major theme. And the blues loves AABA. Typically the chord structure entails the simple chordal movement of one, fours, and fives, such as in the key of C with C, F, and G chords, or the key of B^b with B^b, E^b, and F chords. What is critical in this simple form is that after the major theme phrases are experienced twice, there arrives a counter melody with a shift of root and alteration of melody sequence that provides a clear harmonic move. Then the shift back to the original theme line represents the decisive turn, or peripeteia— because now the original theme line is no longer the same.

"What a Friend We Have in Jesus"

"What a Friend We Have in Jesus" makes it clear. Hymns often simplify the plot, beginning with a claimed resolution—only to introduce trouble, conflicted by means of the middle section called the bridge.

> A – What a friend we have in Jesus,
> All our sins and griefs to bear!
>
> > *—now that's clear...*
>
> A – What a privilege to carry,
> Everything to God in prayer!
>
> > *—of course, but...*
>
> B – O what peace we often forfeit,
> O what needless pain we bear,
>
> > *—which suggests the reason...*
>
> A – All because we do not carry,
> Everything to God in prayer.

The bridge not only changes the harmonic progression of the music, it also inserts a strangely conflicting lyrical content, with the result that the concluding return to A becomes altogether different. In short, this decisive turn happens, not only by means of the melody line and harmonic structure—its musicality—but also by means of the content of its lyrics. The B portion is the double troubling portion that prompts the reversal.

This, however, is not the last shift. There is also a radical shift of content within the several stanzas being sung. This is the larger progression of Begbie's illustration.

Perhaps you may recall times when the liturgist decided the service was running late and needed adjustment by limiting time for singing the last hymn. So the liturgist suggests omitting one of the four stanzas. If only three will be sung, the liturgist chooses, of course, for the congregation to sing stanzas 1, 2, and 4. Guess what is left out when stanza 3 is excluded? Why, the conflicted turnaround stanza. A couple of illustrations show the damage:

"Holy, Holy, Holy"

1. Holy, holy, holy! Lord God Almighty!
    Early in the morning our song shall rise to thee.
    Holy, holy, holy! Merciful and mighty,
    God in three persons, blessed Trinity!

    —indeed . . .

2. Holy, holy, holy! All the saints adore thee,
    Casting down their golden crowns around the glassy sea;
    Cherubim and seraphim falling down before thee,
    Which wert, and art, and evermore shalt be.

    —oh yes, but now big trouble . . .

3. Holy, holy, holy! Though the darkness hide thee,
    Though the eye of sinful man thy glory may not see,
    Only thou art holy; there is none beside thee,
    Perfect in power, in love and purity.

    —yet nonetheless . . .

4. Holy, holy, holy! Lord God Almighty!
   All thy works shall praise thy name, in earth and sky
     and sea,
   Holy, holy, holy! Merciful and mighty,
   God in three persons, blessed Trinity.[24]

Without the third stanza the song turns pale—true, but powerless. Or, again, "Joy to the World, the Lord Is Come!"

"Joy to the World, the Lord Is Come!"

1. Joy to the world, the Lord is come!
   Let earth receive her King;
   Let every heart prepare him room,

   _____

   And heaven and nature sing. *(repeat twice)*
   And heaven, and heaven, and nature sing.

   —*indeed . . .*

2. Joy to the world, the Savior reigns!
   Let all their songs employ,
   While fields and floods, rocks, hills and plains
   Repeat the sounding joy. *(repeat twice)*
   Repeat, repeat, the sounding joy.

   —*oh, but . . . uh oh . . .*

3. No more let sins and sorrows grow
   Nor thorns infest the ground;
   He comes to make his blessings flow

Far as the curse is found. *(repeat twice)*
Far as, far as, the curse is found.

—*nonetheless* . . .

4. He rules the world with truth and grace,
    And makes the nations prove
    The glories of his righteousness,
    And wonders of his love. (*repeat twice*)
    And wonders, and wonders, of his love.[25]

No wonder David Robb, "with apologies to Joyce Kilmer," has written this "Ode to the Third Stanza":

I think that I shall never see
A resurrected stanza three:

The third, with oft the salient thought
revealing why the hymn was wrought;

The third which sometimes bares the soul
the hymnist wanted seen as whole:

The third, replaced by interlude
through which we stand in somber mood;

"Let's sing the first, the second and the last,
the way we've done it in the past!"

Hymns are sung by folk like me,
But only God sings stanza three! [26]

Denouement

Oliver Wendell Holmes once said, "I wouldn't give a fig for the simplicity that exists on this side of complexity, but I would give the world for the kind of simplicity that exists on the other side of complexity." [27] I think he might be willing for us even to include the shape of content within stanzas 1, 2, 3, and 4.

Now we get released into the future. Aristotle called it denouement, opening into the future. I think of Jacob's lifetime journey. I'm sorry to say the lectionary stopped the chosen series too soon—stopped just short of denouement. The lectionary series on Jacob stops at the backside of the Jabbok River. Too bad.

You recall Jacob nearly perfected the art of the con job: He received home schooling on the subject, which prompted him toward long and quick journeys; thought he had even conned God with a self-serving ladder; finished an internship at his uncle's place; and now is finally heading home, only to be alerted that his brother, even after all these years, is coming toward him with an army of four hundred, but, fortunately, is still some distance away—on the other side of the Jabbok River.

Jacob's large entourage—wives, servants, children—as well as over a hundred animals of all kinds provide big gifts to present to his brother. Call that bribes. He divides everybody and all the livestock into two groups and sends them all over to the other side of the river—the Esau side. He instructs them to say when confronted by Esau, "Here are gifts from your servant, who is behind us." Yes, indeed, I should say, *here are bribes from your enemy, who is behind us, way behind us,* lodging on the safe side of the Jabbok. Well, he thought it the safe side.

But a divine figure arrived in the night for a wrestling match. They wrestled all night long, and Jacob got his hip put out of joint. The text suggested that Jacob "prevailed." Well, that doesn't mean prevailed over God. The text clarifies the meaning by way of his later remark when he said, "I have seen the face of God and am still alive." He prevailed all right: over death.[28]

The lectionary committee allowed the story to cease right here, but note the next portion of the story. Next morning Jacob gets up with a new name and crosses the Jabbok River. He is limping, of course, because of the hip out of joint. Ah, but he is whole for the first time. He has been running for two decades, but now he doesn't need to run anymore. And what does he do? He passes by both groups he had put in harm's way, past the wives, past the children, past the servants, past the bribes—taking his place up front. Now he will be the first to face his angry brother with an army of four hundred. They meet, and they embrace with tears.[29] That's called denouement. It opens into a future made altogether new.

Another feature of the concluding denouement needs naming. This final focus ought not be ended with the heaviness of oughts, shoulds, and musts. Better for these "therefores" to be surrounded by the good news of the gospel. Fred Craddock does it so well. Instead of having the final words represent what we now must do, he moves beyond the "therefores" with a flashback to the good news already named. The result is to place brackets around our necessary response. And hence, the sermon makes it clear that finally the central focus of the message is not human obedience after all, but rather the power of God's grace that undergirds the possibility of human response. I call it the half-reprise.

You may be familiar with how the big band often finishes its presentations. Just when you think the final note is sounded, someone in the silence shouts out, "One more time." With that, the band replays the last few bars of the song—maybe even twice. Craddock's half-reprise is that after clarifying the call of the gospel, he goes back to the most powerful moment of the announcement of the power of God—and names just a part of it. Having already heard its power, *we* finish the gospel word while Fred is taking his seat behind the pulpit.

Leroy Ostransky noted that what distinguishes great jazz musicians from ordinary ones is "not the eloquence of the final resolution, but the profundity of the prior irresolution."[30] Which is to say that ordinary musicians produce musical tension the resolution of which is so obvious that the listeners know where things are going before the musicians actually play it out.

Unfortunately, we have all heard sermons like that—with listeners finishing before the preacher. For us, it is to say that the powerful closing eloquence of the sermon is not what makes for great preaching. The desired profundity can happen only on the strength of the depth of the prior sermonic tension.

Conflict, Complication, Peripeteia, and Denouement

These are the stages of classic tragedy literature, the marks of musical sequence, and the moves we can make when we encounter the Aristotle Blues—with the decisive turn made by means of the gospel.

"When the Saints Go Marching In"

In 1938, Louis Armstrong cut a record of "When the Saints Go Marching In." Strangely, he began the recording with spoken words: "Good evening, brothers and sisters. This is Reverend Satchmo coming at you with a mellow sermon for the evening." At first hearing, I thought, isn't that clever? But it wasn't clever; it was profound. You see, he knew something I had not yet learned about jazz. When the call and response modality of the African American congregation moved out onto the secular street and turned into jazz, people knew that the trumpeter was in the role of the preacher as the leader of the call and response improvisation. He indeed *was* the reverend.

And he continued, "We take as our text, 'When the saints go marching in.'"

That is—after all—precisely the eschatological reality that beckons all that preachers do.

RECOVERING THE VOICE OF ORALITY

Aristotle has helped us discover how a plot works, from issue to answer, from conflict to resolution—always moving thought forward, beat after beat. But there is yet more to the subject of homiletical narrative strategy, of facilitating the movement. It is crucial to note that for preachers this movement in time happens by means of oral address—by means of mouth-to-ear communication, *not* hand to eye.

Fred Craddock has warned us about the dangers of ignoring this distinction.

> Let a preacher begin thinking that the point is to get Sunday's sermon written, and a string of negative results follow. In the first place, the written sermon is a kind of closure which offers not only a sense of satisfaction—thank God, I'm finished with it!—but also a shutting down of germination and gestation, often prematurely.[1]

The consequence, concludes Craddock, is that "to make writing the sermon the goal of the process is to cause one to think writing, rather than speaking, throughout the preparation."[2] Fred Craddock is not against writing, but he understands it as a servant toward the goal of oral speech called the sermon. "To say a sermon is oral," he continues, "is not to say simply that it is spoken but that it is prepared with principles of orality closely observed."[3]

Walter Ong clarifies this radical distinction further. As he said in the Terry Lectures on the campus of Yale University some years back, "Spoken words flow . . . are free moving," even "fleeting . . . [but] what is written stays put . . . It is a record."[4]

Indeed, writing loves complete sentences properly produced, of good grammar—privileging the nouns, of course. Rather than a verb-based language such as Hebrew, the Greco-Roman–type languages privilege nouns and the stasis they suggest. Hence, we move toward resolution, marked by a big fat period at the end of the written sentence. No wonder gestation and germination may, in fact, close down. Oral speech, on the other hand, loves the kind of run-on sentences that facilitate ongoing consideration.

Several years later, Walter Ong noted in another writing that with print it's even worse. "Print is comfortable only with finality," he said, and hence "the printed text is supposed to represent the words of an author in definitive or 'final' form."[5] This sense of moving toward "final form" is precisely why the period is geared to shut down thought.

Of course, the monumental differences between literality and orality are played out at multiple levels: *contexts, sources, experiences,* and *consequences* of ongoing thought. The bottom line, however, is that the dominant mode of speech is *time*; the dominant mode of writing is *space*. Space as typically experienced has to do with settledness; time as typically experienced has to do with movement. Written words lean toward separation; spoken words lean toward inclusion.

This difference, as so articulately described by Ong—how written language moves toward closure while spoken language moves toward openness—is especially noteworthy when occurring in the context of conflict.

I remember something my dear friend and fine colleague, Dr. Tex Sample, said to me one time a number of years ago. I must have been involved in some kind of institutional conflict that now I cannot recall. But I do remember what Tex Sample said: "I know you feel strongly on this subject." No doubt he was correct—and so he explained his concern: "I don't know how you are going to communicate your views, but I have a suggestion for you and that is, whatever you do, do not put it in writing, because if you do there is very little wiggle room from there on. When you put it down, it's done." Exactly. Said Walter Ong: "Writing 'retains' words. This, indeed, is its raison d'être. . . . It holds words so that they do not escape."[6]

Speech, on the other hand, is remarkably different. Kirk Byron Jones, in his wonderful *The Jazz of Preaching*, notes that "the mysterious common ground of jazz and preaching is this: one never ever arrives. Their wells are always deeper; there is always more."[7] Working aloud respects the fact that there is always more.

Improvised Orality, Double-track Thought And the Committee Meeting.

Moreover, it is crucial to notice the remarkably differing dynamic of the phenomenon of speech when actually in the mode of *improvised orality.* Such speaking involves a double-track of thought, between what is actually being spoken at that moment and that which, coterminously, is being noticed silently—for the sake of the next sentence. Indeed, while one sentence is being delivered, another is being considered. While the mouth is moving, part of the speaker's mind is focused on what is *not* included in the mouth's exposition until the next sentence. Writing tends to do the exact reverse.

Perhaps you have experienced all of this in a meeting— many times over. And you have met this participant—in several forms. We will call him Bill. It is a very important meeting, and Bill is present. Unfortunately, Bill is altogether too eager, too vocal, and hence is becoming an impediment for the group's engagement with the crucial business at hand. He is eager to get his two cents' worth in—which is precisely the level at which others have evaluated his contribution.

Heather, the conveyor of the meeting, takes Bill aside at the first break and says, "Bill, thank you so much for coming today, and for the contributions you've made thus far in our meeting. Now, in order to facilitate greater participation of all those present, I urge you to be a little more timid, a bit more reticent, about how many times you offer your views. In fact, it would really be good if you could resist making a contribution until you actually know what it is that you want to say." Asked Bill, "Well, how will I know what I think until I hear myself say it?"

Although Bill is probably not the best candidate for the preaching ministry, he still represents all of us one way or another—whether we are preachers or not. This is so, not because our contributions are worth only two cents, or that we have some propensity toward being overeager. Our connection runs deeper than that—whatever our gifts and graces. It is this sheer fact that spoken words tend to prompt additional thought on the part of the speaker as well as the listeners. The mind is literally thinking about both what the lips are saying and what you might want them to say in the next sentence. Both happen at once.

For example, somebody interrupts you with a question about subject X. But recently your mind has been engaged with the consideration of subjects Y and Z. Although you have a residual sense of understanding about subject X, it has not been on your mind lately, and, hence, at this moment crisply articulated words are not available. So when the question is posed about your views on X, you respond, "Well, you have caught me a bit off guard here, but, well, I'll give it a try." And you say, "Seems to me, yada, yada, yada," and then quickly add, "Oh no, no, no, that's not quite what I mean; let me try that again. Yada, yada, YADA, Yada—oh, and well, of course, you know there are a couple of exceptions to this principle, and you must remember that it may depend on the context in which the situation is found." It is natural for you inwardly to be considering what in fact you are not saying in the current sentence. This phenomenon is constantly going on in oral communication. With writing or print, the further thought happens after you have already read what you wrote.

One way to couch this enormous difference between print for the eye and voice for the ear is to say that what you see is *out there*, and what you hear is *in here*. Utterly different. As you are no doubt aware, each can sometimes trump the other—that is, *seeing* and *hearing* have different points of power. In part it depends on the context.

When Writing Trumps Speaking: The Board Meeting

For example, there is a board meeting. You've been given the responsibility to provide the persuasive speech for this important advance in the work of the organization. You've worked hard to get a powerful speech ready. You also have a fact sheet prepared and handy, hoping that by the time people get on board for the possibility of entertaining this wonderful future that your speech is helping them imagine, you are prepared *then* to show that in fact, the group can do it. You have given explicit instructions about when to distribute the fact sheet.

Unfortunately, by the time you are in about sentences eleven, twelve, and thirteen, you discover somebody did not hear your instructions and they've started handing out the fact sheet. Well, you know what happens. The group will not hear a word you say for the next ten minutes. The reason is that the fact sheet is in front of their face. Some will be reading one section of data, others focusing somewhere else. And then there is the sweep of focus by those who never did like the idea to begin with. Quickly they look for the reason they will be able to rebut the whole proposal—once your "persuasive" speech is over.

Well, you had just as well stop the speech and go through the fact sheet. But now it is in the wrong sequence. (You do notice the term here: *sequence*.) You'll never be able to regain the power that you would have had, had you been able to keep your speech moving on to completion.

As Walter Ong explains, "If the speaker asks the audience to read a handout provided for them, as each reader enters into his or her own private reading world, the unity of the audience is shattered, to be re-established only when oral speech begins again."[8]

So after you go through the entire fact sheet, you say, "Well, as I was saying earlier"—and you go back to a now impoverished speech—impoverished because the unity of the audience has been shattered.

In this particular case, the eye wins, but at another, far deeper level, you will find the reverse is altogether the case.

When Speaking Trumps Writing: The Lone Ranger

Back when I was a child, I used to listen to the Lone Ranger on radio. And oh, how wonderful was that plot. Every time, of course, the Lone Ranger wound up saving the world. However, as I now reflect on the show, the Lone Ranger had to be saved regularly by Tonto. That Tonto was always present suggests that in fact the hero was not "lone." As Justo and Catherine Gonzáles remind us, Tonto was part of an ethnic minority and, therefore, did not count. (They had to change the name when they sent the program south of the border because the word *Tonto,* as pronounced correctly in Spanish, means "dimwit.")[9]

Yet the "Lone" Ranger wins the day, gets on his horse, and the William Tell Overture cranks up. Oh, it is so bold; it's so noble! It is wonderful! Oh, and the horse! The steed galloping beneath the Lone Ranger as he goes out! What a magnificent creature. Into the distance they go, with our hearing the question: "Who was that masked man?" Indeed, the overture, the horse, and the story were all equally noble.

One generation later I walk through the room that has the television in it and my children are watching the Lone Ranger show. I stop to watch. Oh, yes, the plot is just as good as it was before and will move to an equally noble conclusion. Sure enough, Tonto saves the Lone Ranger, the Lone Ranger saves the world, and goes riding off to the beat of the bold William Tell Overture. But you wouldn't believe the puny pony that's underneath the Lone Ranger. It should have been retired long ago.

How is it that I might notice the difference? How could such a perception occur? Well, when you prompt imagination by means of spoken orality, the mental picture that is evoked is most likely far more powerful than someone might see on the back of a bulletin or on a screen up front. It prompts what we can and will bring to the moment—and in this case is *interiorly present* not just *exteriorly produced* and hence is far more powerful because it has the inside track. But the issue at hand is larger yet. I face it often.

Having been invited as guest preacher for Sunday, I head toward my task. Arriving at the church, I glance at the bulletin that includes the text and sermon title that I had sent in advance. In perusing the bulletin I notice that on the back page they have printed the biblical text on which my sermon will be based. (Or the text will be projected onto the chancel screen later.) I am not pleased. What some might think is a double chance for the congregation to become familiar with the text, I see as a conflict of media. I do not want people receiving the text by means of pale print, either on the back of a bulletin or up on the screen. I want the human voice to be able to shape how the Word is heard.

I have experienced yet another way that reception of the text is badly diluted. Sometimes the bulletin instructs the congregation to "turn to page 127 in the New Testament pew Bible." Let me explain the unfortunate result by means of a brief biblical example.

You recall that in the call of Simon as the Lukan version remembers it, Jesus experiences the sunrise on the shore of the Sea of Galilee. Having borrowed a boat, he is about to preach. The people are gathering at that natural amphitheater. More and more people are coming; they want to hear the Word. Finally the assembly has become a shoulder-to-shoulder event—people packed solidly together. Is it possible that the reason Jesus needed a boat was that the crowd became so large he might just get pushed into the water? (Shoulder-to-shoulder listeners; I suppose that's every preacher's dream!)

When Jesus completes his message, he turns to Simon and says, "Put out into the deep water and let down your nets for a catch."[10] That is the most absurd request you could possibly imagine. Can he not see that the fishermen along the shore of the Sea of Galilee—all are washing their nets? Why are they all washing their nets? Because it is morning. Because the sun has come up. Their "day's" work is done when the sun comes up. Doesn't Jesus know about fishing? This is not a good text for him not if he doesn't know much about fishing.

The text only provides two sentences of Simon's response to the request. Surely one cannot imagine that he had only two sentences to say in response. He had to have said more than that. I can imagine his saying something like, "You do see the nets being cleaned by all the other fishermen around here, and you surely know why. Now, you're a good talker, Jesus, and we love to hear your stories. But, I'm a fisherman and I'm a pro and I know when to fish and when not to fish."

Well, I don't know whether he said all that, but he should have if he didn't. At any rate, the text gives us only two sentences of response—the first of which says: "Master, we have worked all night long but have caught nothing."[11] Do you hear the reproach in the voice? It doesn't appear in the print. But you can hear it in a reader's voice. The reading of the text at this point could have the capacity to embody the startling "distance" just now prompted between Jesus and Simon. The text offers only a period. And a long pause in the reading just now could help immensely. Most important, the sense of that distance will empower the early movement of the sermon.

Then comes the utter resignation of the second line, when Simon says: "Yet if you say so, I will let down the nets."[12] The New American Standard Bible presents the mood more strongly: "But I will do as You say."[13] Do you hear it?

This is no time to allow the corporate power of speaking and hearing to be diluted by the weakness of private reading in a crowd of people. (Recall Ong's rendering of this kind of situation.) So I do not want the congregation to look at print here—each one at her or his own speed. I want all to be engaged with this crucial moment of dialogue. Moreover, there are yet more such problematic situations.

There also is the business of the "fill in the blanks" section of a larger Sunday bulletin. Sometimes it will remind the congregation about how little we remember of what we hear— and it certainly will instruct the congregation to fill in some blanks provided in the bulletin while the sermon is in progress. Perhaps the new pastor is really eager for you to jot down this word or that phrase that summarizes an important moment in the message. So obediently you try to oblige—and you keep half listening, half looking, and missing a good bit of what is being said. "Oh, there's the sentence! Oh, no, guess not." And then, "Oh, this is it, yes, yes!" By the time you get it written down, well, the preacher is ten to twelve sentences further on. You'll be lucky to catch up.

Why do things like that happen? Because some people think the primary goal of the sermon is informational recall. A significant side effect of literality is the hope that writing something down will help trap the idea. But trapping for the purpose of later recollection is not the goal of a sermon;

evoking a meaningful congregational event *now* is. As Henry Mitchell identifies it, every sermon must have a behavioral aim, "matching behavior as well as belief."[14] Says Brueggemann: "The event of preaching is an event in transformed imagination."[15] It is the kind of speech that "destabilizes all our settled 'facts,' and opens the way for transformation."[16] For David Buttrick, the stated purpose for the sermon is to form corporate consciousness in the congregation in that hour.[17] "A sermon," Craddock emphasized, "is not only to *say* something but to *do* something."[18] *These* are the goals for preaching—far different from a word-retention goal. Oh, the human voice, the potential power of the human voice.

Leonard Sweet notes that "the ears, not the eyes, are the gateway. . . . Sight transforms the world into an object. Sound treats the world as a subject. Sight is distancing. Sound is enveloping."[19] Ong has it right that "sound unites groups of living beings as nothing else does."[20] Writing, on the other hand, provides "distance from lived experience."[21] Indeed, most of the time the writer writes alone, and although many may read the writing, most will be reading alone as well. On the other hand, the speaker shares *with*. Since, as Ong notes, "Print encourages a sense of closure, a sense that what is found in a text has been finalized, has reached a state of completion,"[22] I say: "Every time you put a period on a page, watch out! It says 'we're done,' and maybe we don't really want to be done just yet."

The Advance of Technology?

At this point, it is interesting to note one of the current turns of technology. For the purpose of communicating at long distances we used to utilize the Morse code on telegraph systems. Then we got telephone lines that began to show up everywhere in the "developed" world. Then phones were produced that could be unattached to the base so that we could walk all around the house while talking on the phone. Then came the cell phone. Oh, the blessed cell phone. Now you can hear your beloved from almost anywhere. And, powerfully, you can hear the nuanced sound of the voice. Even if a dear one is asking a difficult question, "why did you do that?" the timbre of the voice shares the floor of affection that lies underneath the question. You can also hear the angularity of a parishioner who is unhappy. Multiple levels of connection happen all at once. But, sorry to say, some levels of connection are unwanted by many. Some prefer distance. And technology now makes it possible. You can now text the message on your cell phone and stay clear, free from vulnerable immediacy with the other. When you are asked a question via text message, you can take your time shaping the right response. No quick improvisation is necessary.

Yet, apparently, texting is not as fast as Morse code. There have been several tests around the world recently in which experts in Morse code and experts in texting vie to see who can successfully transmit a paragraph of information the quickest, and in every case Morse code has won. Seems to me a kind of reverse technological evolution, don't you think? (And some have to pay extra for the privilege of texting.)

Jay Leno asked Billy Crystal: "Do you Twitter?" His reply: "No, I can talk."[23] So Fred Craddock and Walter Ong join Billy Crystal in noting the enormous corporate power of the human voice. As Craddock has reminded us, "writing is for reading, and speaking is for listening."[24] My concern is that this important focus on orality must include not just the actual presentation but also all the steps of preparation.

Sermon Preparation: Text after Text, Time after Time

Having explored briefly the typical differences between the activities of speech (orality) and the activities of writing (literality), it is time to explore more concretely the preaching office in terms both of sermon preparation *and* sermon presentation. The goal is to prompt the recovery of the voice, indeed the voices of orality for preaching.

It is crucial to notice that the more profoundly powerful influences on our preaching are those we *do not* notice. We do pretty well with the variables close at hand, naturally noticed and easily identifiable. But our automatically held tendencies that we take for granted without knowing or naming—these are the powerful forces at work for Sunday. Regarding the sermon, it is not enough just to know the differences between orality and literality while speaking. Remember Craddock's fervent instruction, that the sermon must be "prepared with principles of orality closely observed."[25] But do we really know the principles we are actually using as we speak?

For example, after crucial focus on biblical grounding for the sermon as well as the preparation of important written sermonic notes—all in the context of our pastoral role—we head toward Sunday morning. Can't we now just leave the world of study, prayer, and preparation, the world of manuscript and print, move to the oral-aural event come Sunday . . . and just "let it fly"? Well, it's not likely.

It is not likely because the manuscript text taken into the pulpit is but the very last of all the texts involved in the sermon preparation process. It is simply the final *coup de grâce*. These other texts also have operated in the modality of textuality. They have groomed us to think in the language of literality— not orality. (This is exactly what caused Craddock to warn us.)

Lectionary Texts

To begin with, many of us start with the three-year *Revised Common Lectionary*. It provides four texts for the worship service, of which typically the preacher selects one for the sermonic base. (While it is not regularly done in my tradition, some preachers combine or interweave more than one of the lectionary offerings in the sermon.) Now, if writing loves closure, and print is satisfied only with finality, you can be sure that the typical lectionary selections will crave fixity even more.

There are exceptions, of course, but the stated doxological principle behind the lectionary selection process generally results in summary conclusions for the offered texts. Note that the first use for *The Revised Common Lectionary* as given by The Consultation on Common Texts, is to "provide whole churches or denominations with a uniform and common pattern of biblical proclamation."[26] Do you hear the implied mandate in that description? It is to provide a "uniform, common pattern"!

And have you noticed there are often gaps in the selections? They may have included verses 1 through 6 and 12 through 18. If so, what happened to verses 7 through 11? Well, perhaps something really interesting or problematic that they don't want you to notice. (And, in fact, you don't have to notice it. You can buy one of those books that have all four texts listed together. They will not highlight the gaps, so you will not have to notice. And, in fact, you can just read all four texts together from one page.)

Regarding these gaps in the lectionary selections, Joey Jeter of Brite Divinity School said it best:

> When verses are missing from a lectionary text it's most often because the missing verses are trouble and the lectionary does not like trouble. It is not designed for preaching per se; it is designed for worship, and each service of worship is to be complete in and of itself, offering a holistic experience of the gospel truth for the day. Discordant texts with interior or proximate conflicts are often either edited or ignored.[27]

Further Lectionary Textual Resources

Besides the chosen lectionary text or texts, typically the pastor has at hand several books or journal publications focused intentionally on whatever Sunday in the Christian year happens to be coming up. Note, these are several texts based on the lectionary texts for Sunday. Typically, they will be happy to bring quick resolution to the presumed points of the biblical texts being utilized.

I have heard that some preachers—eager to not spend too much preparation time for the Sunday sermon—will actually perform an Internet search for other people's sermons or sermon outlines—texts on this very text. More texts yet. (Often one will discover that this "borrowed" sweat appears not to have had much sweat at the other end.)

Again, most of these texts have lured us into the mode of literality that will bring us to closure way too soon. Often the result prevents openness to the world around us—a world that otherwise might provide powerful and even juxtaposed embodiment for the biblical source.

Nora Tisdale shares the story of a fascinating homiletical project. A researcher chose three cities and interviewed twenty-four pastors regarding their sermons on the first Sunday after the beginning of the Gulf War of 1991. The questioning had to do with how they dealt with that world event in the preached sermon. Most of the pastors reported that they did not say anything about it, because they "follow the lectionary."[28] Well, if you don't include crucial world events in your preaching, you are not likely to notice much that happens in the parish either.

Further Lectionary Issues

My complaints regarding the results of the lectionary committee's selection process go beyond my concern about its penchant for resolution. A few examples will reveal some of the range of my concerns and can be better understood by means of a few examples.

Daniel 7:1-3, 15-18

The All Saints Day Hebrew Scripture selection for Year C is quite revealing. Their choice of the book of Daniel for this special Sunday immediately suggests several wonderfully available choices for hearing what sainthood really means. You recall some images that could work powerfully. Included in Daniel are accounts of the fiery furnace, a den of lions, and the courage of civil disobedience from which to choose. But these are not chosen for All Saints Day, Year C or otherwise.

Oh, and one could have focused on the scene of that sumptuously loaded banquet table that the Babylonian king offers to the young, best, and brightest vanquished victims of war. Yes, with courage they choose veggies and water instead. What saintly power that is—called by Daniel L. Smith-Christopher in the *New Interpreter's Bible* the "cuisine of resistance."[29] At least the lectionary choosers might have offered us the picture of courageous faithfulness in forbidden prayer while the enemy is looking in the window. That could really preach in our celebration of the saints. But no, none of the above passages were chosen.

Instead, they selected Daniel 7:1-3 and 15-18. Verses 1-3 mention the four beasts in the water. But let me tell you, the lectionary committee is not really interested in the beasts. Had they been interested, they would not have left out verses 4 and beyond—the verses that explain the meaning of the beasts. Instead they jump to verses 15-18. Verses 15-17 provide a "neat" segue from the beasts to verse 18 that then declares "the saints of the Most High shall receive the kingdom." But why would they jump there? Could it be that somebody did a computer word search and typed in the word *saints*? Well that was the older Revised Standard Version (RSV) rendering (as well as the New International

Version [NIV], 1984 edition). But the wording in the New Revised Standard Version (NRSV) has been changed to read: "the holy ones of the Most High shall receive the kingdom."[30] So, if you are using the NRSV, likely you will never know why the committee chose these verses. Again, why couldn't they have given us the picture of those sneaky spies peeking through the window into resolute faithfulness? I do not know, but instead they chose for us an otherwise bland term, and left it at that. Clearly, we are unable to be certain about the committee's reasoning, but my bet is that it has something to do with desiring a touch of closure for the special day—one that does not raise any biblical eyebrows about justice or courage.

Micah 5:2-5a

This text is chosen for Advent 4, Year C. The lectionary committee appears to be certain those verses are referencing the coming of Jesus. One must put aside the work of biblical commentators that suggests a different meaning altogether, related to the context of the Exile and hoped-for return to a restored Jerusalem. My hunch is that the text arrives during Advent by means of the inclusion of the term *Bethlehem*. The cry against those who "devise wickedness / and evil deeds on their beds," and who after morning comes, "covet fields and seize them; / houses, and take them away,"[31] is sorely missed. The oppression of "householders" and even "their inheritance"[32] could find a new context for the advocacy of justice in today's pulpit had this passage been chosen.

2 Samuel 6:1-5, 12b-19

This selection for Proper 10, Year B, is calculated to provide a wonderfully smooth transition of power for David by bringing the ark of the covenant into Jerusalem. But the committee had to delete the egregious self-serving strategy of David to bring it off. Hence, they simply omitted verses 6 through 12a, which reveal how David first refused having anything to do with the ark because he was afraid it was too risky and then later asked for it after hearing the blessing that another received when it was in his care. It is difficult to imagine a worse illustration of proof-texting. And they did not finish the story with Michal's stinging rebuke of David's outrageous behavior!

Galatians series, chapters 1 through 6

The several passages of Galatians that are chosen are not bad—yet reveal an unfortunate lectionary selection mentality—as has already been named by Joey Jeter. Certainly the committee has included important theological concerns of Paul's work in Galatia. Yet, a close look will reveal the whens and wherefores of those passages that are chosen, and the consistent avoidance of passages that involve powerful embodied conflict.

In particular, there is a set of six successive Sundays in Year C, Propers 4 through 9, that move through the book of Galatians. (Note the exception of chapter 4 that is listed for Holy Name Sunday A, B, C, and Christmas 1-B.) This selection process for these six sequential Sundays produced a fine beginning, choosing the first twelve verses of chapter 1, that makes clear why Paul is writing to them, why he is gravely concerned, and what is needed for correction. Recall that unlike his usual beginning words of praise in other Pauline epistles, the Galatians letter avoids any opening praise. Rather, it jumps to: "I am astonished that you are so quickly deserting the one who called you in the grace of Christ."[33] It is a good passage, setting the stage for the next five Sunday selections.

But, again unfortunately, most of the time we do not get to hear this opening selection that includes Paul's strong rebuke, because Pentecost and Trinity Sundays take precedence over the selection. So, when this text comes up in 2013, it will not have been included in the series for eighteen years. In fact, most of the three-year sequences of the lectionary will not include Galatians 1:1-10 at all.

Most of the three-year cycles will pick up Galatians 1:11-24—where Paul describes his background, his Damascus road experience, and his first brief trip to Jerusalem three years after his conversion. It is a mild-mannered selection, no large issues here. But note what does *not* happen with most of chapter 2 that tells his version of his relationship with Jerusalem. Just when Paul's conflict with the leaders in Jerusalem is about to become explicit, we are left in the dark.

The committee does not include the escalating theological controversy central to Paul's letter. Not only is the account of his second trip to Jerusalem after fourteen years left out— you may recall that he put it strongly: "We did not submit to them even for a moment!" Why? "So that the truth of the gospel might always remain with you."[34] Did someone once say that Paul had made contact with others immediately after his conversion? Paul continues the reference to his relations with "those who were supposed to be acknowledged leaders

... those leaders contributed nothing to me."[35] Now, that's heady stuff, and apparently too much for us to hear. More surprising still—and continuing in this unused section of the Galatian letter, the theological fight at Antioch is absent altogether. This is when Peter "stood self-condemned," and "even Barnabas was led astray by their hypocrisy."[36] What a remarkable moment! How could anyone exclude this centerpiece to the entire letter?

Here you have Simon Peter and Paul, the two largest figures in this new Christian movement, conflicted over what is central to the gospel. Indeed, this is a conflict still alive in powerful ways to this day. But we were not invited to attend. Instead, we read something about those who have been named much later by scholars as the Judaizers—but here they are left nameless and faceless—an easy mark when left unembodied.

Moreover, there is a larger reason why this Antioch conflict passage ought to be included in our preaching here. The passage speaks not only about the specific issue at stake; the passage makes a point about theological diversity inside the New Testament text and era. Is it too much to expect personally named conflicting points of view?

The continuing part of Galatians 2 that is included in the lectionary selections elaborates on the theological consequences of being "justified by faith in Christ."[37] This is important to recognize, of course, but with the lectionary editing process it misses the conflict that gives it power. Unfortunately, by means of deletion it is an answer to an absent issue.

And now comes the bombshell of chapter 3! We hear it in the very first verse: "You foolish Galatians"; or as J. B. Phillips calls them, "dear idiots"; or as the New English Bible puts it, "stupid." The Jerusalem Bible asks simply: "Are you people in Galatia mad?" This is heavy indeed, after which Paul asks: "Did you experience so much for nothing?"[38] Ah, you can't do that on Sunday, can you? Apparently not. The committee elected to set it aside. And besides that, here the law is called a curse. Unfortunately, Galatians 3:1-22 is not included. The lectionary passage begins again with verses 23-29, where the law is now imaged in a different tone, as temporary "disciplinarian."[39]

Five verses of the fourth chapter are included in the lectionary at another place in the cycle. Included there is the notion of our being children adopted as heirs by God. *Not included* four verses later is Paul's remark of frustration: "I am afraid that my work for you may have been wasted,"[40] and then later asking: "Have I now become your enemy by telling you the truth?"[41] What *is* included and what *is not* included reveal a strong tendency to stay with the even-keeled portions and exclude the more roughly conflicted passages. Therefore we will not be surprised to discover that when Paul's apparent exasperation bubbles over with "I wish those who unsettle you would castrate themselves!"[42] it does not get included in the lectionary selections. Too strong; too strong! The included portions of chapter 5 are verses 1 and 13-25, which involve Paul's admonition to live by the Spirit. (Note the excluded verses where he boldly assails "You who . . . have cut yourselves off from Christ.")[43]

The final chosen passage in this series comes from chapter 6. It includes Paul's call for gentleness toward anyone involved in some transgression, and then a fairly strong concluding passage of admonition, including his warning that "God is not mocked, for you reap whatever you sow."[44] Finally, he concludes that "neither circumcision nor uncircumcision is anything; but a new creation is everything! As *for those who will follow this rule*—peace be upon them!"[45]

The two final verses of the letter, however, are not included: "From now on, let no one make trouble for me; for I carry the marks of Jesus branded on my body," and "May the grace of our Lord Jesus Christ be with your spirit, brothers and sisters. Amen."[46]

All in all, this particular editorial work results in avoiding the sharpness of the conflict, muting the proclamatory power, and turning Galatians into a modest piece of instruction. It could have been so much more.

Jonah 3:1-5, 10—including some expository assistance

The lectionary committee's approach to Galatians pales in comparison to the price of such editing in the case of the story of Jonah. The editorial treatment of Jonah is much more severe—more like an amputation. As a result, it deserves closer examination—including a review of some writings intending to provide expository assistance for preachers who want to use this lectionary passage in their sermons.

The one major selection of Jonah in the lectionary involves Epiphany 3 Sunday, Year B. (There is an additional Sunday selection, Proper 29, Year A, with an additional portion of verses from Jonah 3 and 4, but these serve only as optional choices—and, meanwhile, suffer the same fate.)

The basic selection of the book of Jonah begins at chapter 3:1. Chapter 3? Where are chapters 1 and 2? Nowhere. Not given is that first call of God that Jonah promptly dissed—the conflict upon which the entire story is based. They took the fundamental itch out, the presenting quandary! We don't have any disobedience! You know, Jonah is supposed to go north and east to Nineveh, but he fled south and west to Tarshish instead. Oh, and now there is no water, no storm, and no sailors—who, ironically, are praying to their gods. Remember, Jonah is asleep in the bottom of the boat. Please tell me, who's the religious leader on this trip?

The story is being enriched with every phrase, but all of this is missing. And remember when Jonah said, "Pick me up and throw me into the sea; then the sea will quiet down for you."[47] Yet the sailors, fraught as they were with the fright of a perilously rocking boat, initially cannot bring themselves to do the deed. Instead, they continue throwing cargo overboard—but to no avail. They cannot reach the shore. Finally they oblige, and, heave ho, they throw him off the ship and he hits the water. Wow, judgment rendered—judgment he had coming. Oh, but there's more than judgment. There is also mercy—because just as Jonah hits the water a celestial seagoing taxicab comes along that gobbles him whole. The very moment when judgment is rendered, grace is offered. Oh, that will preach. But no, they left it out.

Jonah probably did not consider his experience with the fish one of grace. He offered a prayer—a very self-serving prayer—in which he said, "As my life was ebbing away, / I remembered the LORD."[48]

Nonsense. His life was ebbing away and God thought of him. That's different altogether. Well, finally, of course, as we know, the fish vomits. You might say the fish repents. (As a matter of fact, everybody repents in this story, except Jonah—the Ninevites, and even God. But we are ahead of ourselves.) The fish vomits Jonah out onto the beach. We are at the book of Jonah, chapter 3, verse 1. And this is where the lectionary has chosen to "begin" the story? It is hard to believe.

The reading of the words "The word of the LORD came to Jonah the second time" is the very first line of the Scripture read that Sunday. God calls; Jonah goes. No issue here—made smooth by deletion. He heads into town—three days wide and one day in—and begins yelling. Notice what he does not say. He does not mention God. He does not mention sin. He does not mention judgment. All he says is "forty days and you're out of here."[49] And folks begin to repent.

Then comes the intervention of the king—well, not for the lectionary committee. They stop the passage just before the king arrives in the text. Note that in verses 6, 7, 8, and 9, the king rises from his throne, removes his robe, covers himself with sackcloth and ashes and proclaims a fast—even including the animals. (I presume that would include sackcloth and ashes for all the dogs and cats—and no food or drink either.) Apparently, the king becomes the resident theologian. "Who knows," he says, "perhaps this may not be God's last word."[50]

But alas, the congregation will not hear these verses read; they are stricken from the record. The chosen text jumps from verse 5 to verse 10. Nor will they hear about Jonah's attitude about God's gracious decision. The lectionary text stops one period-mark before the Scripture says: "But this was very displeasing to Jonah, and he became angry."[51] The selection does not even mention Jonah's response! How can this be?

We might recall that instead of this evangelist being thrilled by such confession from such an obviously unlikely group, in fact he was so angry he wanted to die—after telling God in no uncertain terms how much and why. We may happen to remember, but the congregation is not privileged with this crucial information today.

Understand, Jonah knew his theology well, and wanted none of it . . . for them. Hated the very thought of it. Which is why he disobeyed to begin with. The empowering fact of grace, the womb-like sustaining mercy, and the enduring nature of steadfast *hesed* love—all this for the Ninevites? He already knew about them—had even read about them in history class. He wanted to die.

But the committee, having already deleted the first two chapters, does not want to bring that up now.

You know there is something about this story that sounds incredibly contemporary, but the lectionary does not give us that part of it. Indeed, that the committee would purposely choose to cut it up this way—and amputate the most important and interesting parts of this powerful story—is to turn the good news available here into pale, pious religiosity. It could have been a powerful word of rebuke for the hatred in our time, but the committee thought otherwise.

Lectionary-based Resources for Preaching— A Really Mixed Bag

Having noted some of the tendencies of the lectionary, its use of the Hebrew Scriptures, its tendency for deletion of conflictive material, its editorial leanings toward flat, instructive affirmations of the gospel, and its penchant for closure, it might be useful to look briefly at a few of the many texts of helpful supportive material—found in lectionary journals and volumes based on years A, B, and C—as well as located from Internet sources. These are, shall we say, *more texts yet—texts* on the lectionary *text* in order to develop *a text* for Sunday morning. Meanwhile, orality is losing the preparation stage to literality by limps and losses.

I decided to explore various lectionary material designed for this lectionary pericope. I examined over twenty available resources. Based on this work, shared below, one might easily conclude that if you want even more closure than we have already exposed in this writing, you will find it in these resources.

Understand, there were a few wonderful offerings working against the grain of the lectionary modality, against the press of print, and, rather, moving toward the vantage of the voice. Four issues emerged.

First of all, what do you do with the missing chapters of the Jonah story? Most interpreters just avoided that fact, one way or another—but not Elizabeth Achtemeier, the late great. She knew exactly what to do. She said, "In order to bring the congregation to the point at which the morning text begins, it is necessary for the preacher briefly to recount the story that precedes our text."[52]

Note that she said, recount the story, not barely mention. And notice also, she did not say, "Recount the story that precedes the preacher's text." Oh, no! She said, "that precedes *our* text." You see, Achtemeier already imagines she is in church. Oh, wow— she's there, fully there! But most commentary writers just avoided or barely mentioned the gap.

One said that Jonah didn't want to go. Another said, "This is a story relating reluctance and now finally submission." There's their sermon. Not likely a good one. One commentator was happy to have avoided any mention of the fish that might "detour" the preacher's focus. One-fourth of the group said nothing about what was missing, and half of the rest said either one sentence or only two regarding chapters 1 and 2.

The second problem was the reduction of the work to flat, cursory summary statements. For example, one said this is the story of repentance. Would we ever have guessed? Another offered four possibilities for the theme but only provided one sentence for each of the four. On the other hand, one publication involved an essay on this text that lasted over eight hundred words but in which the name *Jonah* was the subject of a sentence only once.

Third, several tangential detours were provided. One said that fishing for converts is the theme here. Another thought serendipity was the central subject, while yet another believed Jonah was fish bait. One writer thought the issue here had to do with the creed.

Finally, particularly striking was that among these twenty-some lectionary commentaries on this text, so many were lacking direct connection to the parish or the world. Several writers were quite good with their exegetical work but were not historically relational. One had references to Jeremiah, Jeroboam, and Elijah, but not with the rest of us. Once again, it was Elizabeth Achtemeier, with her ear to the life of the congregation, who in her very first sentence said: "Anyone who still holds the old stereotypical opinion that the God of the Old Testament is wrathful and judgmental in contrast to the God of the new, who is loving and merciful, should carefully study the book of Jonah."[53] Oh, yes indeed. That remark will get our minds off the page and into consideration.

On the other hand, J. Howard Wallace of the faculty at Uniting Church Theololgical Hall, Melbourne, Australia, in an ongoing lectionary commentary series, connected the Jonah text to our time by noting that we live in a "world where serious voices, be they religious, political, economic, or military, would tell us why we cannot break the boundaries we've set up to keep others at a distance." On the other hand, "God's disarming humor . . . challenges every life-denying limitation set by human hands, with its infectious joy."[54] Oh, yes, he knows how to connect.

Out of more than twenty lectionary sources that I perused, a few were really quite helpful. But most were dull, offering obvious ideas not enlivened by the depth of juxtaposition or the reach of particularity. We should be reminded again by Brueggemann's powerful observation that "the deep places in our lives—places of resistance and embrace—are not ultimately reached by instruction."[55]

I do believe in lectionary use for its important liturgical purposes as congregations live through the movements of the

Christian Year. But here too, worship must not be reduced to information-gathering as a primary goal.

Therefore . . .

What can we do with the lectionary, besides use it? We watch it. We watch it very carefully! We must be aware of the ways it wants closure and finality—desiring avoidance of the kind of juxtaposition in which preaching is launched. I think we need a fourth year that includes material that's not now included, because—as currently provided—the lectionary is a pretty narrow canon. This is so, not just by what is not included at all, but often by how the lectionary committee members have shaped what has been selected.

At stake in all of this is the crucial concern about functioning in the mode of orality throughout the preparation process. And text after text after text lures us into literality that wants to end consideration and further thought. It wants completion that can close the mind down with a very settled period-mark.

The Sound of the Sermon

A further word regarding the tension/resolution modality may be helpful. It is important to remember the numerous forms that the tension-resolution modality involves—some brief and multiple and some large and encompassing. If the tension-resolution modality is limited to a series of same-paced "little-blips," they become tiresome. My use of Aristotle's plot is not simply about repeated dyads of tension and resolution; it has to do with the overall movement of the plot. The bad turns worse, the expectation grows ever larger, until a sudden shift occurs toward the resolution of the whole. Remember Jeremy Begbie's comparison, how musical tension-resolution segments occur at different levels and spans at the same time, resulting in incredible musical variety, all following the same principle but involving particularly diverse manifestations. So it is with the ongoing beat of the sermon.

What is crucial is to recover the sound of the sermon, to keep the acoustical affair acoustical—to read out loud, to think out loud, to write out loud, to work out loud. Literally, every biblical text for worship should be experienced in numerous translations out loud so our ears can hear what the text is saying and what we hope to share again. It means that before the preacher begins to put pencil to paper or hand to computer keyboard, to actually, literally, hear what one is about to write in order to hear what one hopes others might bother to hear. Because when one writes first and then hears, likely it is too late for the preacher to really listen to what will show up on Sunday.

For instance, one of the great preliminary things to do when traveling in the car is to paraphrase a text out loud. Practice embodied speech. I'm talking about finding ways regarding lingering and listening and looking. It moves the beat forward, empowers sermonic orality, and deepens the forward-moving proclamation.

It was on November 14, 2008, ten days after the national election. Bill Cosby was the guest of David Letterman, and after the comedic part of the program they sat down together. Letterman asked: "Could you share with me about your day on the day of election?"

Now, one might think how others trot out the usual, such as, "You know, this was a historic moment." Indeed, millions have said that. Or Cosby certainly could have reported, "I was quite emotional about it." Thousands have said that. Surely, he might have said, "I never thought it would happen in my lifetime." Many others have said that. Why didn't he do that? Well, because of the language with which Bill Cosby works. Here's what he said.

> Well, I was at my desk and I reached for the frame of a picture of my father and took the picture out of the frame and put it in my pocket. (He gestured) I reached for the picture of my mother, pulled it out of its frame and put it in my pocket. (Gestured again) They're both dead now, you know. Then I reached for the picture of my younger brother who died at the age of six. I was seven at the time, and put his picture in my pocket. (Gestured again) Then he said, "I took the pictures to the polls and once the curtain was pulled behind me, I put the pictures out in front of me. I put them out and I said . . . 'Now, *we* are going to vote.' "[56]

What a picture of the practice of imagination with particularity. Joseph Sittler observed that "imagination is not addition; it's always evocation." As Sittler articulated it, "Imagination is the process by which there is reenacted . . . the salvatory immediacy of the Word of God as . . . witnessed to by the speaker."[57] As mentioned in chapter 2, that's what Barbara Brown Taylor was doing when she had the Samaritan woman move out of the light and then Jesus move into the light. She was putting action to the ideational movement of the text itself.

Principally, we have been dealing here with the narrative principle of preaching, noting that every sermon moves from moment to moment, beat by beat—one way or another—literally keeping time with the Word. It is the sheer facticity of temporal sequence that time after time sermons move forward by means of the strategies of suspense, the potential embodied forms that it takes, the sounds that it makes. Moreover, the clear mandate is to practice mouth-to-ear communication, not hand to eye. Keep the homiletical beat beating.

And don't forget to delay resolution. We've heard it already from Haddon Robinson, that when the tension is gone, "the sermon is over."

Yes, when the tension is gone, it *is* over. And so is this writing.

NOTES

1. Introduction

1. Henry Grady Davis, *Design for Preaching* (Philadelphia: Fortress Press, 1958), p. 163.

2. Ibid., pp. 163–64.

3. Stephen H. Webb, *The Divine Voice: Christian Proclamation and the Theology of Sound* (Grand Rapids: Brazos Press, 2004), p. 51.

4. Davis, *Design for Preaching*, p. 164.

5. Ibid., p. 168

6. Kirk Byron Jones, *The Jazz of Preaching* (Nashville: Abingdon Press, 2004), p. 30.

2. The Three Levels of Narrativity

1. Richard L. Eslinger, *A New Hearing* (Nashville: Abingdon Press, 1987), p. 65.

2. Henry Grady Davis, *Design for Preaching* (Philadelphia: Fortress Press, 1958), p. 163.

3. Ibid.

4. Ibid.

5. William Herbert Perry Faunce, *The Educational Ideal in the Ministry* (New York: Macmillan, 1908), p. 170.

6. Davis, *Design for Preaching*, p. 164.

7. Fred Craddock, *As One Without Authority* (Enid, Okla.: The Phillips University Press, 1971), p. 52.

8. John Ciardi and Miller Williams, *How Does a Poem Mean?* (Boston: Houghton Mifflin Company, 1975), p. 6.

9. Thomas G. Long, *Preaching from Memory to Hope* (Louisville: Westminster John Knox Press, 2009), p. 2.

10. Ibid., p. 3.

11. Ibid.

12. Ibid.

13. Ibid.

14. William H. Willimon and Richard Lischer, eds. *Concise Encyclopedia of Preaching* (Louisville: Westminster John Knox Press, 1995), p. 342.

15. Long, *Preaching from Memory to Hope*, p. 4.

16. Ibid.

17. Jess Stein, ed., *The Random House Dictionary of the English Language*, Unabridged Edition (New York: Random House, 1967), p. 890.

18. Long, *Preaching from Memory to Hope*, p. 7.

19. Ibid., p. 12.

20. Ibid.

21. Davis, *Design for Preaching*, p. 163.

22. Ibid., pp. 139-62.

23. Craddock at Lutheran convocation on preaching in Florida.

24. Thomas Long, "Plotting the Text's Claim Upon Us" in Don M. Wardlaw, ed., *Preaching Biblically* (Philadelphia: The Westminster Press, 1983), p. 87.

25. Craddock, "Story, Narrative, and Metanarrative," in Mike Graves and David J. Schlafer, eds., *What's the Shape of Narrative Preaching?* (St. Louis: Chalice Press, 2008), p. 88.

26. Fred Craddock, *Preaching* (Nashville: Abingdon Press, 1985), p. 167.

27. Graphic is from Jeremy S. Begbie, *Theology, Music and Time* (Cambridge: Cambridge University Press, 2000), p. 161.

28. Ibid., p. 30.

29. Ibid., p. 104.

30. Ibid., p. 106.

31. Ibid., p. 183.

32. Haddon Robinson, Audio Workshop Interview, Preaching Today.com.

33. Frederick Buechner, *Telling the Truth* (New York: Harper & Row, 1977), p. 7.

34. Begbie, *Theology, Music and Time*, p. 38.

35. Craddock, *Preaching*, p. 166.

36. Ibid.

37. Walter Brueggemann, *Finally Comes the Poet* (Minneapolis: Fortress Press, 1989), p. 4.

38. Ibid., p. 5.

39. Ibid., p. 13.

40. Ibid., p. 43.

41. Ibid., p. 79.

42. Ibid., p. 111.

43. Eugene L. Lowry, *The Homiletical Plot, Expanded Edition* (Louisville: Westminster John Knox Press, 2001), p. 71.

44. Paul Scherer, *The Word God Sent* (New York: Harper & Row, 1965), p. 7.

45. Sallie TeSelle (McFague), *Speaking in Parables* (Philadelphia: Fortress Press, 1975), p.16.

46. Craddock, *Preaching*, p. 196.

47. Ibid., p. 199.

48. Gabriele Lusser Rico, *Writing the Natural Way* (Los Angeles: J. P. Tarcher, 1983), p. 187.

49. Brueggemann, *Finally Comes the Poet*, p. 3.

50. Eugene L. Lowry, *How to Preach a Parable* (Nashville: Abingdon Press, 1989), p. 80.

51. Ibid.

52. Ibid., p. 82.

53. Ibid., p. 83.

54. Buechner, *Telling the Truth*, pp. 8–9.

55. Ibid., p. 21.

56. Long, *Preaching from Memory to Hope*, p. 34.

57. Barbara Brown Taylor, "Reflections on the Lectionary," *Christian Century*, February 12, 2008 (Vol. 125: No. 3), p. 19.

58. Brueggemann, *Finally Comes the Poet*, p. 9.

59. Taylor, *Christian Century*.

60. Joseph Sittler, *The Ecology of Faith* (Philadelphia: Fortress Press, 1961), p. 46.

61. Eugene L. Lowry, *The Homiletical Plot* (Atlanta: John Knox Press, 1980), pp. 5-100.

62. Eugene L. Lowry, *Doing Time in the Pulpit* (Nashville: Abingdon Press, 1985), pp. 69–74.

63. Ibid., p. 76.

64. Michael Polanyi, *Knowing and Being* (Chicago: The University of Chicago Press, 1969), p. 133.

65. Lowry, *The Homiletical Plot*, expanded edition, p. 119.

66. O. Wesley Allen Jr., ed., *The Renewed Homiletic* (Minneapolis: Fortress Press, 2010), pp. 81–92.

67. Thomas H. Troeger, *Imagining a Sermon* (Nashville: Abingdon Press, 1990).

68. Isaiah 6:1-5.

69. Troeger, *Imagining a Sermon*, pp. 39–40.

70. Ibid., pp. 44–47.

71. Craddock, *Preaching*, p. 167.

3. Encountering the Aristotle Blues

1. The Lyman Beecher Lectures at Yale in 2009 and the William Self Lectures at Mercer/McAfee in 2011 inform this chapter. At Yale, I was joined by two other musicians, Mr. Mac McCune of Branson, Missouri, trumpeter, and the Reverend Carlos Summers of Conway, Arkansas, trombonist. The purpose was to utilize music

in a jazz idiom to help translate Aristotle's views regarding plot for the sake of grasping the significance of the narrative principle in the art of preaching.

2. H. Grady Davis, *Design for Preaching* (Philadelphia: Fortress Press, 1958), p. 164.

3. Ilion T. Jones, *Principles and Practice of Preaching* (New York: Abingdon Press, 1956), p. 71.

4. Eugene L. Lowry, *Doing Time in the Pulpit* (Nashville: Abingdon Press, 1985), p. 64.

5. The audio recording at http://www.abingdonpress.com/the-homiletical-beat/ will demonstrate.

6. Luke 24:9.

7. Luke 24:13.

8. Helmut Thielicke, *The Waiting Father* (New York: Harper and Brothers, 1959), p. 27.

9. David J. Schlafer, *Surviving the Sermon: A Guide to Preaching for Those Who Have to Listen* (Cambridge: Cowley Publications, 1992), pp. 63–76.

10. Dorothy Fields and Jimmy McHugh, "On the Sunny Side of the Street" (New York: Shapiro, Bernstein & Co., 1930).

11. Philippians 3:13b-14.

12. Philippians 1:25.

13. Philippians 1:21.

14. Exodus 32:7-8, paraphrased.

15. Exodus 32:9-10.

16. Exodus 32:11, italics added.

17. Exodus 32:12.

18. Exodus 32:14.

19. George A. Buttrick, *Jesus Came Preaching* (New York: Charles Scribner's Sons, 1931), p. 140.

20. John 3:2-3, paraphrased.

21. John 3:3 KJV, paraphrased.

22. John 3:4, paraphrased.

23. John 3:8, paraphrased.

24. *The United Methodist Hymnal* (Nashville: The United Methodist Publishing House, 1989), 64.

25. *The United Methodist Hymnal*, 246.

26. David A. Robb. Selah Publishing Company.

27. Unknown source; sometimes cited with the words "give my right arm" rather than "the world."

28. See Genesis 32:1-31.

29. Genesis 33:1-4.

30. Leroy Ostransky, *The Anatomy of Jazz* (Seattle: University of Washington, 1960), p. 83.

4. Recovering the Voice of Orality

1. Fred B. Craddock, *Preaching* (Nashville: Abingdon Press, 1985), p. 190.
2. Ibid.
3. Ibid., p. 169.
4. Walter J. Ong, S.J., *The Presence of the Word* (New York: A Clarion Book, Simon and Schuster, 1967), p. 93.
5. Walter J. Ong, *Orality and Literacy* (London: Routledge, 1988), p. 132.
6. Ong, *The Presence of the Word*.
7. Kirk Byron Jones, *The Jazz of Preaching* (Nashville: Abingdon Press, 2004), p. 41.
8. Ong, *Orality and Literacy*, p. 74.
9. Justo L. González and Catherine G. González, *The Liberating Pulpit* (Nashville: Abingdon Press, 1994), p. 50.
10. Luke 5:4.
11. Luke 5:5.
12. Ibid.
13. Luke 5:7 NASB.
14. Henry H. Mitchell, *Black Preaching: The Recovery of Preaching* (New York: Harper & Row, 1977), p. 147.
15. Walter Brueggemann, *Finally Comes the Poet* (Minneapolis: Fortress Press, 1989), p. 109.
16. Ibid., p. 5.
17. David Buttrick, *Homiletic Moves and Structures* (Philadelphia: Fortress Publishers, 1987), p. 320.
18. Craddock, *Preaching*, p. 200.
19. Leonard Sweet, *Summoned to Lead* (Grand Rapids: Zondervan, 2004), p. 57.
20. Ong, *The Presence of the Word*, p. 122.
21. Ong, *Orality and Literacy*, p. 42.
22. Ibid., p. 129.
23. *Tonight Show*, May 28, 2009.
24. Craddock, *Preaching*, p. 192.
25. Ibid., p. 169.
26. *The Revised Common Lectionary* (Nashville: Abingdon Press, 1992), p. 9.
27. The Academy of Homiletics, "Papers," 2007, pp. 6-15.
28. Leonora Tubbs Tisdale, *Preaching as Local Theology and Folk Art* (Minneapolis: Fortress Press, 1997), p. 101.
29. Daniel L. Smith-Christopher, "Daniel," in *The New Interpreter's Bible*, vol. 7 (Nashville: Abingdon Press, 1996), p. 37.
30. Daniel 7:18.
31. Micah 2:1-2.
32. Micah 2:2.
33. Galatians 1:6.
34. Galatians 2:5.

35. Galatians 2:6.
36. Galatians 2:11-13.
37. Galatians 2:16.
38. Galatians 3:4.
39. Galatians 3:25
40. Galatians 4:11.
41. Galatians 4:16.
42. Galatians 5:12.
43. Galatians 5:4.
44. Galatians 6:7.
45. Galatians 6:15-16, italics added.
46. Galatians 6:17-18.
47. Jonah 1:12.
48. Jonah 2:7.
49. Jonah 3:4, paraphrased.
50. Jonah 3:9, paraphrased.
51. Jonah 4:1.
52. Elizabeth Achtemeier, *The Lectionary Commentary*, Roger E. Van Harn, ed. (Grand Rapids: William B. Eerdmans Publishing Company, 2001), p. 486.
53. Ibid., p. 484.
54. J. Howard Wallace, Online Biblical Resources.
55. Brueggemann, *Finally Comes the Poet*, p. 109.
56. *CBS Late Show*, November 14, 2008.
57. Joseph Sittler, *The Ecology of Faith* (Philadelphia: Muhlenberg Press, 1961), p 56.